Phineas and Ferb

BIG BOOK of SCIENCE EXPERIMENTS

By Cody Crane

Based on the series created by Dan Povenmire and Jeff "Swampy" Marsh

SCHOLASTIC INC.

ISBN 978-0-545-48195-3

Based on the series created by Dan Povenmire and Jeff "Swampy" Marsh

Copyright © 2013 Disney Enterprises, Inc.

Text copyright © Scholastic Inc.

All rights reserved. Published by Scholastic Inc.

SCHOLASTIC and associated logos are trademarks and/or registered trademarks of Scholastic Inc.

12 11 10 9 8 7 6 5 4 3 2 1   13 14 15 16 17 18/0

Printed in the U.S.A.   08

First printing, February 2013

Designed by Carla Alpert

Contents

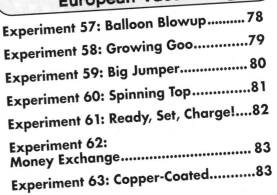

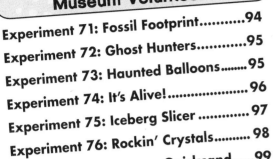

WEEK ELEVEN: Museum Volunteers

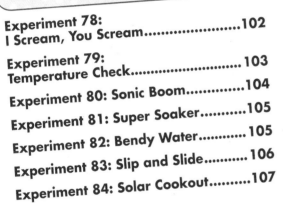

WEEK TWELVE: Heat Wave

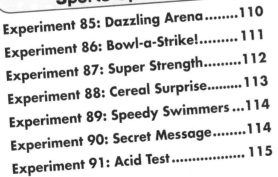

WEEK THIRTEEN: Sports Spectacular

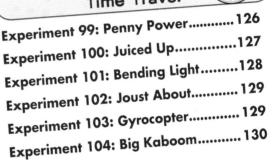

WEEK FOURTEEN: Superstars

WEEK FIFTEEN: Time Travel

Get Ready for
The Best Summer Ever!

School's out for the summer! No more homework and no more tests to study for. What are Phineas Flynn and his stepbrother, Ferb Fletcher, going to do? They are determined to have the best summer vacation ever!

The boys plan to spend every day of vacation working on science experiments and coming up with over-the-top inventions. Phineas and Ferb usually work in their backyard lab in Danville, a major city in the Tri-State Area. You, too, can hop over and join in on the fun!

This book contains 104 experiments—one for each day of summer vacation. Each one helps Phineas and Ferb put their big ideas in motion. You'll use science to make things whirl, zoom, fizz, splat, and sometimes EXPLODE! At the end of each week, you'll find a helpful chart to keep track of the experiments you've done, plus more cool activities to keep you busy.

Are you READY to GET STARTED?

Now that you're on the way to Phineas and Ferb's backyard, there are a few things you must know. Not everyone is a fan of Phineas and Ferb's science experiments.

The boys must keep their eyes peeled for **Candace**, their older sister. Candace is always trying to bust her brothers by revealing their latest creation to their mom. Aside from that, Candace is just like any normal teen girl. She likes hanging out with her friends, learning to drive, and flirting with her crush, Jeremy.

A bigger threat to the boys is **Dr. Heinz Doofenshmirtz**, an evil mastermind. (Although Phineas and Ferb don't know about him.) He's constantly coming up with strange inventions to wreak havoc on the Tri-State Area—and the world.

Luckily, there's someone ready to put a stop to his schemes. It's Perry, Phineas and Ferb's pet platypus.

Perry acts like a low-key animal when he's around his owners, but watch out! He leads a double life as **Agent P**, a crime-fighting secret agent. Agent P reports to Major Monogram, head of the O.W.C.A. (Organization Without a Cool Acronym). Agent P makes sure that Dr. Doofenshmirtz's evil plans don't stand a chance!

Shh . . . Geniuses at Work

What's that? You don't hear anything? That's because Phineas and Ferb have their thinking caps on. They are coming up with ways to make sure that their experiments go off without a hitch. This way, they can have lots of fun and avoid getting caught by Candace.

If you want your experiments to go just as smoothly, follow these simple lab rules:

- **Stick to the steps outlined for each project.** Changing the steps might cause the experiment to fail. It could be dangerous, too.

- Some experiments call for an adult helper. **Don't attempt these projects on your own.**

- **All experiments can be done with common household objects.** Make sure to ask an adult before you use any of these items.

- Look like a scientist! **Protect your eyes by wearing safety goggles** during experiments. You can find a pair at your local hardware store.

- Dress like a lab genius! **Wear an apron or old T-shirt to protect your clothes.**

- **Cover your work area** with newspaper to avoid a mess.

- **Wash your hands** before and after each experiment.

- **Keep pets and little kids safe from your experiments.** Make sure they stay away from your work area.

- **Clean up when you are done.** That way, your work area and tools will be ready for the next experiment.

- **Don't smell, eat, or drink the ingredients** or the results of your experiment. (That's unless the instructions say that it is okay to do so.)

- **All waste liquids can go down the drain.** Rinse the sink out by letting the faucet run. Solid materials, including semi-solid things like gel and slime, go in the trash.

Get Some Lab Partners!

Experiments work best when you have friends to help you out. These kids always lend Phineas and Ferb a hand!

Isabella Garcia-Shapiro is the boys' friend and neighbor. She is very capable and organized. It's no wonder that she's the leader of Fireside Girls Troop 46231. She's determined to earn lots of new accomplishment patches for her troop!

Phineas and Ferb can also depend on **Baljeet**—if it won't get in the way of his studying. Baljeet moved to Danville from India to get a good education. He loves math and is always doing calculations. Baljeet thinks getting a "B" on a math test would be the scariest thing ever!

Who's this big guy? He's **Buford Van Stomm**. He may always pick on Baljeet, but he is really a softy at heart. He's always up for helping the gang!

Phineas and Ferb have tons of big ideas, and they can't wait to get started. Let's put on some lab gear, gather all the equipment, and get busy!

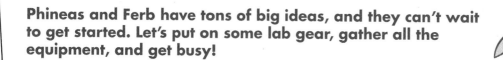

A Couple More Things . . .

- If you ever come across a word in **bold** and don't know its meaning, look it up in the glossary starting on page 133.

- And if you ever come across Dr. Doofenshmirtz, keep your head down, act busy, and don't let him know what's going on. *Shhh* . . .

Backyard Laboratory

It's the first week of summer vacation. Yay! So long, alarm clocks, gym class, and homework! It's time to start having fun! First, Phineas and Ferb feed Perry. Then they head outside for some fresh air. The boys sit under the tree behind their house and start dreaming up new inventions—like a machine that blows enormous bubbles, a device that shoots out rainbows, and how to combine summer and winter!

Mega-Bubbles

Phineas and Ferb celebrate the first day of summer vacation by blowing festive bubbles! These aren't normal bubbles, though. The boys build a bubble-making machine that pumps out bubbles that are large enough to trap Perry inside! Let's blow some big bubbles.

What You Need:

- Two straws
- 4-foot-long piece of string or yarn
- Large pan
- 1/2 cup corn syrup
- 1 cup dishwashing liquid
- 3 cups water

What You Do:

1. Thread the string through the two straws.

2. Tie the ends of the string together.

3. Mix up some bubble solution by adding the corn syrup, dishwashing liquid, and water to the pan. (Save your leftover bubble solution for the next experiment!)

4. Dip your straw-and-string contraption into the bubble mix. With one hand holding each straw, form a hoop. Gently remove the hoop from the mix.

5. Carefully walk backward and watch a mega-sized bubble form!

Warning! This experiment can get messy. Do it outdoors.

What's Happening Here?

A bubble is an air pocket trapped inside a thin film of soapy water. When you walk, air pushes on the soapy film, causing it to stretch out from your hoop. But when it breaks free, the soapy film comes together to form a ball. That's because this shape takes up the least amount of **surface area** and uses the least amount of energy to form. Adding corn syrup to your bubble solution helps make the film extra stretchy. That allows you to make big bubbles that are not so easy to POP!

Crazy Foam

What's just as fun as big bubbles? Millions of tiny ones! Phineas and Ferb change the setting on their bubble machine. Instead of giant bubbles, the device now pumps out lots of little ones that stick together as foam. The boys fill the backyard with lots of fluffy stuff! Let's join the fun!

What You Need:

- Small plastic soda bottle
- Scissors
- Washcloth
- Rubber band
- Bubble solution from page 12

Warning!
You need an adult helper for this experiment. This experiment can get messy. Do it outdoors.

What You Do:

1. Have an adult helper use scissors to cut off the bottom of the bottle.

2. Cover the bottom of the bottle with the washcloth. Use the rubber band to hold the cloth in place.

3. Dip the washcloth in the bubble solution.

4. Blow slowly through the top of the bottle. YIKES! It's a giant foam snake!

What's Happening Here?

The washcloth is full of tiny holes that act like miniature bubble wands. As you blow through the bottle, air squeezes through the holes. The result: thousands of tiny bubbles. The substances in the bubbles' soap film are attracted to one another. That's why the tiny bubbles stick together to form blobs of foam. Your fingers may be too large to pop the tiny bubbles one by one. No worries! The bubbles will eventually disappear. Just wait for the water in the soapy film surrounding the bubbles to **evaporate**.

Rainbow Maker

Hey, it's Isabella. She always asks, "Whatcha doin'?" Today, Isabella mentions that she has never seen a rainbow. Phineas and Ferb decide to build a device that shoots a band of colors across the sky. Isabella can't wait to see her first rainbow!

What You Need:
- Shallow, clear rectangular pan
- Water
- Small mirror
- Sunny spot or flashlight
- White paper

What You Do:

1. Fill the pan with water. Then prop the mirror inside the pan against a side.

2. Angle the pan so sun shines directly on the mirror. (If it's not sunny enough, shine a flashlight onto the mirror instead.)

3. Hold the piece of paper above the side of the pan across from the mirror. Adjust the paper and the mirror until the light coming up from the water hits the paper. Ooh . . . pretty!

What's Happening Here?

As sunlight **reflects** off the mirror and up through the pan of water, rainbow colors appear on the piece of paper! Sunlight may look white, but it's actually made up of a spectrum of colors, most noticeably: red, orange, yellow, green, blue, indigo, and violet! As the light passes through the water, it **refracts** and separates into its many different colors. A real rainbow forms in a similar way when sunlight strikes tiny water droplets in the air.

Spiky Ice

Summer is great, but so is winter. Phineas and Ferb combine the two seasons into a new one: S'Winter. In this mix-up season, icicles grow upward instead of down!

What You Need:
- Distilled water
- Ice-cube tray
- Freezer

What You Do:
1. Fill a clean ice-cube tray with distilled water.
2. Place the tray in the freezer.
3. Wait overnight and remove the tray. Wow, spikes!

What's Happening Here?

An ice cube freezes from the outside in. Water also expands as it freezes. As the cube freezes toward the center, expanding ice forces water in the middle to move upward. As the water pushes up, it freezes into a spike. Minerals in tap water prevent ice spikes from forming. Distilled water is mineral-free. So, spikes!

Freeze Ray

Warning!
This experiment can get messy. Work over a sink.

The boys decide to ice skate in S'Winter. They invent a freeze ray that zaps a kiddie pool into ice. Check out this instant freezing action!

What You Need:
- Small bottle of soda water
- Refrigerator
- Large bowl
- Ice
- Water
- 2 cups salt

What You Do:
1. Put the soda bottle in the refrigerator.
2. After 3 hours, fill a large bowl with ice and a little water. Sprinkle in two cups of salt.
3. Place the bottle into the ice water for 10 minutes.
4. When time's up, hold the bottle over a sink.
5. Slowly twist off the bottle's cap. Watch as the liquid transforms into ice!

What's Happening Here?

The bubbles in soda come from carbon dioxide. This gas also lowers the drink's **freezing point**, making soda freeze at a colder temperature than water. When you open the bottle, you hear the *WHOOSH* of carbon dioxide escaping. As the gas gushes out, the freezing point of the super-chilled soda rises. So it instantly freezes.

Secret Sauce

Phineas and Ferb are having an awesome backyard barbecue! They've designed a robot chef that grills up yummy burgers. But what makes the machine work so well is Baljeet's perfectly balanced robot fuel! Let's stir up some more fuel and fill up the robot.

What You Need:
- Glass jar
- 1/4 cup corn syrup
- 1/4 cup water
- 1/4 cup cooking oil
- Spoon
- 1 grape

What You Do:
1. Pour the corn syrup into the jar.
2. Tilt the jar, and slowly pour the water down the side into the jar.
3. With the jar still tilted, slowly pour the oil.
4. Set the jar on a countertop. The ingredients float on top of one another!
5. Now, for the final ingredient, drop in the grape. Does it sink or float?
6. Stir up the sauce. Do the layers stay mixed?

What's Happening Here?

Syrup, water, and oil each have a different **density**. The same amount of each liquid weighs a different amount. The heaviest liquid (syrup) sinks to the bottom of the jar, while the lightest (oil) floats on the top. Water and the grape sit between the two. Stirring up the layers causes the syrup and water to combine. The oil stays separate. That's because water and syrup are **miscible**—they can mix. But water and oil can't!

Fingerprint Scan

Where's Perry? He's off getting the scoop on Dr. Doofenshmirtz. To find out his latest mission from Major Monogram, Agent P heads to his secret lair under Phineas and Ferb's house. A machine scans Agent P's webprint to verify his identity. The door to the hideout opens. Try scanning your thumbprint!

What You Need:

- Drinking glass
- Baby powder
- Clear tape
- Black construction paper

What You Do:

1. Press your thumb firmly against the glass.

2. Gently shake some baby powder over where you pressed your print. Blow off the excess powder.

3. Smooth a piece of tape over the powdered thumbprint.

4. Carefully peel off the tape and stick it to a piece of black construction paper.

5. Examine your print. Can you see swirls and loops in the pattern?

6. Take a friend's or family member's print and compare it to your own.

What's Happening Here?

Your fingerprints are unique to you. You can't find another person on this planet with the same prints! That's why they can be used as identification to get into top secret spaces. Fingertips have swirling ridges of raised skin. Fingers also contain oils. When a person touches an object, oily prints of their fingers' ridges are left behind. For that reason police study fingerprints to catch criminals. In **forensics**, police collect prints from a crime scene using a way that is similar to this experiment!

This Week's Roundup

Way to go! You finished the first week of experiments! Fill in the chart to keep track of the results of your work.

EXPERIMENT		DESCRIBE THE RESULTS OF THE EXPERIMENT
1.	Mega-Bubbles	
2.	Crazy Foam	
3.	Rainbow Maker	
4.	Spiky Ice	
5.	Freeze Ray	
6.	Secret Sauce	
7.	Fingerprint Scan	

Now Try This!

The fun continues. Unscramble the words below. All the jumbled words can be found in this chapter. Then unscramble the highlighted letters to solve the answer to the secret question below. To find the answers, turn to page 136.

1. ROAMJ MGOOMNAR _ _ _ _ _   _ _ _ _ _ _ _ _

2. SCIRFENOS _ _ _ _ _ _ _ _ _

3. ULBBEB _ _ _ _ _ _

4. ITYDSEN _ _ _ _ _ _ _

5. WINABRO _ _ _ _ _ _ _

6. AVPEOARTE _ _ _ _ _ _ _ _ _

Unscramble all the highlighted letters above to answer the top secret question below.

The Secret Question: Isabella is a member of what organization?

_ _ _ _ _ _ _ _ _ _ _ _ _ _ _

Annual Danville Festival

DANVILLE IS GREAT!

Welcome to Danville! Population: 241,000. This town has everything. It has a store that sells blueprints for building inventions, a pizzeria, a bowling alley, a museum, a massive mall, and much, much more. Dr. Doofenshmirtz even has his own organization, Doofenshmirtz Evil, Incorporated, located right in the middle of town!

Every summer, the citizens of Danville throw a festival to honor their hometown. Phineas and Ferb get in on the celebration by building a parade float, making Danville souvenirs, and more!

Parade Float

Warning!
You need a CD for this project. But don't use one without permission. Ask an adult to give you a CD they won't mind if you ruin.

The Danville Festival starts with a parade down the town's main street. Phineas and Ferb have built their own parade float with a science theme. Want to know what's so special about their float's design? This parade float really *floats*!

What You Need:

- Water bottle lid with a pop-up spigot
- Glue
- CD
- Balloon

What You Do:

1. Make sure the spigot of the lid is closed. Then put a circle of glue on the rim of the non-spigot side.

2. Position the non-spigot side over the hole in the CD's center. Let the glue dry completely!

3. Blow up the balloon and pinch the neck so no air escapes.

4. Stretch the neck over the spigot.

5. Place your hovercraft on a flat, smooth surface, like a tabletop.

6. Now, open the spigot. Push the CD and watch your float go. Whee!!

What's Happening Here?

You built a hovercraft! Air flows out of the balloon and under the CD. This creates a cushion of air under the CD, so it floats. Without air, the CD would not be able to move far. That's because it would rub against the surface and generate a slowing force called **friction**. Since your hovercraft floats above the table, it's all smooth sailing.

Green Thumbs

Danville is hosting its annual vegetable-growing contest. Will Phineas and Ferb win? They have a good chance. They are going to make **compost** that will help their tomatoes grow to the size of a house! Let's see how composting works.

What You Need:
- Ripe banana
- 2 sealable plastic bags
- 2 tablespoons water
- Package of dry yeast

What You Do:

1. Break the banana into one-inch chunks.
2. Place half of the banana pieces into one of the plastic bags and half into the other.
3. Squeeze most of the air out of one bag and seal it.
4. Add half of the packet of yeast and the water to the other bag. Then squeeze out most of the air and seal it.
5. Place the bags in a sunny spot.
6. Check on your bananas every day for three days. Compare the bags.

What's Happening Here?

Yeast is a type of **fungus**. Fungi play an important role in nature. They help break down and get rid of dead matter. If you tossed a banana onto a compost pile, fungi would start munching on it. This causes it to **decompose**, like the banana in your bag. The food scrap would eventually become a nutrient-rich compost for fertilizing plants.

Fantastic Plastic

To celebrate their hometown, Phineas and Ferb are going to open a factory to make Danville Festival souvenirs. The factory will make snow globes, mugs, and key chains all molded out of plastic. Each will be printed with the slogan "Danville Is Great!" Time to whip up some plastic!

What You Do:

Warning! This project is messy. Work over a sink.

1. Add the milk and vinegar to a bowl. Stir the mixture and place the bowl in a warm, sunny spot for an hour.

2. Fit a coffee filter into the mouth of the drinking glass. Flip the filter's edge over the glass's rim. Use a rubber band to hold the filter in place.

3. In the sink, slowly pour your milk mixture through the filter. (It may take a few minutes for the liquid to drain through.)

4. Carefully, pour some water through your filter to rinse off the white goop that remains.

5. Place your filter on a couple of paper towels to remove the excess moisture.

6. Mold the goop into a shape. Leave your shape on a piece of waxed paper for a few days to harden. You've got a plastic souvenir!

What You Need:

- 1 cup milk
- 2 tablespoons white vinegar
- Bowl
- Stirrer
- Coffee filter
- Drinking glass
- Rubber band
- Water
- Paper towels
- Waxed paper

What's Happening Here?

Vinegar, an **acid**, causes the milk to separate into two parts: a clear, watery part and a white, goopy part. The goop is a substance called casein. It is a type of **polymer**—the main ingredient in plastics. Some of the first plastics ever created, nearly 100 years ago, were made from milk polymers. Today, the polymers used to make plastics are made from crude oil.

Spin It

Phineas and Ferb build a helicopter to fly a "Happy Danville Day" banner all over the city. Let's crank up the propeller!

What You Need:
- Lightweight cardboard
- Ruler
- Scissors
- Glue
- Pushpin
- Pencil with eraser tip

What You Do:

1. Cut a 6-inch-by-6-inch square piece of cardboard. Then cut a 2-inch-by-2-inch square from each of the four corners of the big square. Fold up the four flaps of paper.

2. With the flaps facing up, glue the center of the cardboard to the pencil eraser.

3. Stick the pushpin through the cardboard's center into the pencil's eraser. Make sure the pin is secure!

4. Roll the pencil briskly between your palms and let go. WHIRL!

What's Happening Here?

As the blades spin, air flows around them. This creates higher **pressure** under the blades than above them. This difference generates **lift**, a **force** that carries the helicopter upward. Your helicopter blades have to spin fast to keep air flowing and stay aloft.

Jump Start

The boys want their helicopter to have a quicker takeoff, so they install a motor. Let's go!

What You Need:
- Index card
- Helicopter from the previous activity
- Tape
- 1-foot-long string

What You Do:

1. Cut a 3-inch-by-2-inch piece from the index card. Wrap the card piece lengthwise around the pencil of your helicopter to form a tube.

2. Make the tube just loose enough so your pencil can turn inside. Tape tube together.

3. Pinch and tape closed the bottom of the tube.

4. Hold the tube in one hand. With the same hand, press one end of the string to the rim of the tube. Use the other hand to wind the string upward around the pencil. (The string shouldn't overlap!)

5. When the string reaches one inch above the rim, quickly pull the string to unwind the "pull-starter."

What's Happening Here?

It takes energy to start your motor. When you wind the string, energy from your muscles transfers to the string as **potential energy**. When you yank the string, the stored energy transforms into **kinetic energy**. The force of the string unwinding sends the helicopter spiraling up! Energy never disappears. It just changes from one form to another.

Wiggling Food

Phineas and Ferb can make anything fun—even dinner! They've opened a new restaurant called Chez Platypus in Danville. The food they are serving is unlike anything that customers have ever seen before. Like this Danville Dancing Pasta!

What You Need:
- Glass jar
- Soda water
- Dried uncooked spaghetti

What You Do:

1. Fill the jar with soda water.

2. Break the spaghetti into 1-inch pieces.

3. Drop the pasta pieces into the jar. Watch that spaghetti boogie!

What's Happening Here?

You learned on page 15 that carbon dioxide gas gives soda its fizz. When you drop spaghetti into the soda water, bubbles of carbon dioxide collect on the pasta. The bubbles are lighter than water so they rise toward the surface. The bubbles carry the spaghetti with them! When the bubbles reach the surface, they burst. This causes the pasta to sink. There you have it, the secret recipe to dancing pasta!

Ooh! Aah!

Time to end the weeklong celebration of Danville with a bang! That means fireworks. But not just any will do. Phineas and Ferb have invented fireworks that explode underwater. The whole town finds a spot to sit back and watch the colorful show. What a BLAST!

What You Need:

- Drinking glass
- Water
- Small bowl
- 1 tablespoon cooking oil
- Blue and red food coloring
- Stirrer

What You Do:

1. Fill the glass halfway full with water.

2. In the bowl, put in the oil, two drops of blue food coloring, and two drops of red food coloring.

3. Stir the oil to break up the droplets of food coloring.

4. Gently pour the oil mixture into the glass.

5. Observe as the food coloring slowly sinks and pops, creating a colorful explosion.

What's Happening Here?

Stirring the food coloring into the oil gives the droplets of color a waterproof coating. When the droplets come into contact with water in the glass, the oil separates and floats on top of the water. (Remember from page 16 that oil and water don't mix.) This releases the food coloring. The color begins to spread out in a process called **diffusion**. The bursts of color look like a fireworks display.

This Week's Roundup

Good job! Another week of projects is in the bag! Fill in the chart to keep track of the experiments you've completed.

EXPERIMENT	DESCRIBE THE RESULTS OF THE EXPERIMENT
8. Parade Float	
9. Green Thumbs	
10. Fantastic Plastic	
11. Spin It	
12. Jump Start	
13. Wiggling Food	
14. Ooh! Aah!	

Now Try This!

Complete this crossword puzzle. Hint: All the clues can be found in this chapter. For answers to this puzzle, go to page 136.

Across
1. Spaghetti is a type of ___.
2. Type of parade vehicle
3. Yeast is a type of ____.
4. Phineas and Ferb's hometown

Down
5. ____ dioxide makes soda fizzy.
6. Material that is made of polymers
7. The ___ in vinegar causes milk to curdle.
8. Phineas and Ferb built a ____ helicopter.
9. Potential and kinetic are two forms of ____.
10. Force that carries a helicopter upward

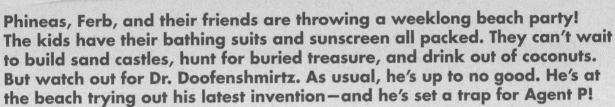

WEEK THREE
Beach Bash

Phineas, Ferb, and their friends are throwing a weeklong beach party! The kids have their bathing suits and sunscreen all packed. They can't wait to build sand castles, hunt for buried treasure, and drink out of coconuts. But watch out for Dr. Doofenshmirtz. As usual, he's up to no good. He's at the beach trying out his latest invention—and he's set a trap for Agent P!

Castle Construction

The beach has miles of sand perfect for building sand castles. Phineas and Ferb want to make one that's as big as an *actual* castle! For their plan to work, their castle's walls need to be sturdy. Phineas and Ferb cook up some special sand that sticks together without toppling over.

What You Need:

- 4 cups flour
- 1/2 cup baby oil
- Rectangular pan
- Different-sized cups

What You Do:

1. Add the flour to the pan. Pour half the amount of baby oil on top.

2. Use your hands to mix the flour and oil together. Try molding the "sand." It crumbles and doesn't stay together.

3. Now add the rest of the baby oil and mix it into your sand. This time, the sand stays together when squeezed.

4. Go ahead and build your sand castle! Use your hands to shape the sand. Also use the different cups as molds.

What's Happening Here?

The flour and oil in this experiment work in a similar way as sand and water at the beach. Dry sand doesn't stick together. Add water, though, and you can squish the sand into all sorts of shapes. Water has a property called **surface tension**. It causes water droplets to want to cling to one another. When water is added to sand, it coats the sand grains. The water coating causes the grains to grab on to others nearby. The result: sticky sand. Getting the right mix of sand and water is the key to a sturdy sand castle.

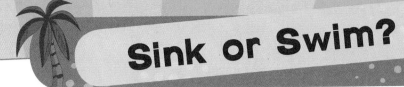

Sink or Swim?

Candace wants to get Jeremy's attention by winning the annual surfing contest. But there's one problem: Candace can't swim! She tricks her brothers into helping her out. Phineas and Ferb fiddle with the water. Now the water will keep Candace afloat—even if she falls in. Check out the boys' handiwork!

What You Need:
- Glass filled with 1 cup of water
- Egg
- 2 tablespoons salt

What You Do:

1. Place the egg in the glass of water.

2. Observe. Does the egg float or sink?

3. Remove the egg. Then stir the salt into the water.

4. Lower the egg into the water. What happens to the egg now?

What's Happening Here?

When you placed the egg in the water it sank to the bottom of the glass. That's because the egg is denser than water. By adding salt, you increase the water's density. Now the egg is less dense than the water and floats to the top of the glass. When an object is less dense than a surrounding liquid, an upward force called **buoyancy** causes it to float. Phineas and Ferb must have added extra salt to the water to help Candace keep her head above water.

Ship Shape

One day Buford decides to help Phineas and Ferb build a sailboat. But he wonders what keeps boats afloat. After all, aren't boats heavier than water? Let's figure this out.

What You Need:
- Modeling clay
- Clear bowl filled with water
- Small objects

What You Do:

1. Roll a ball of clay. Drop it into the water. Watch what happens.

2. Remove the ball of clay from the water. Reshape it into a shallow bowl. Set your "boat" on the water. It floats!

3. Place some small objects in your boat as cargo. How much can it carry before it sinks?

What's Happening Here?

An object's weight doesn't determine if it will float. Boats float because of their shape! The ball of clay sinks because it doesn't **displace** much water. The clay boat weighs the same as the ball, but its **mass** is more spread out. That allows the boat to push aside much more water than the ball. If it displaces an amount of water equal to its weight, it floats!

Buried Treasure

Arrgh, matey! Phineas and Ferb have found a pirate's treasure map, but part of it is missing. Let's build a machine that can find metal objects, like coins, buried underground.

What You Need:
- 10 paper clips
- Paper
- Scissors
- 2 cups cornmeal
- Rectangular pan
- Ruler
- Foot-long piece of string
- Magnet

What You Do:

1. Draw 10 coins on a piece of paper and cut them out. Clip a paper clip to each coin.

2. Put the coins in the pan. Cover them with the cornmeal.

3. Tie one end of the string to one end of the ruler. Tie the other end of the string to the magnet.

4. Hold the ruler above the pan so the string is straight. The magnet should sit just on top of the cornmeal.

5. Drag the magnet over the cornmeal. How much treasure did you collect?

What's Happening Here?

An invisible force called a **magnetic field** surrounds a magnet. This field attracts objects that contain the metal iron. The magnet picks up the paper clips, so they must contain iron! Use your magnet to test to see what household objects contain iron.

Dive! Dive!

The gang has decided to look for the lost ancient city of Atlantis. Legend has it that this city sank beneath the sea long ago. To find the city, the group will have to scuba dive to the bottom of the ocean! They get ready to jump in!

What You Need:
- Large plastic soda bottle
- Water
- Ketchup packet

What You Do:

1. Drop your ketchup packet into the bottle. The packet is your "diver."

2. Fill the bottle to the top with water.

3. Tightly screw on the bottle's cap.

4. The packet should be floating near the top of the bottle. Now squeeze the sides of the bottle. The packet dives down.

5. Let go of the bottle. The packet swims to the surface!

What's Happening Here?

The ketchup packet dives just like Phineas, Ferb, and their friends. That's because it contains a little bit of air inside. This pocket of air allows the packet to float near the top of the bottle. Squeezing the bottle increases the pressure inside the bottle. The force causes the bubble inside the ketchup packet to shrink. This causes the packet's overall density to increase, so it sinks. When you release the bottle, the air inside the packet expands again. The packet's density drops. Up goes the packet!

Sneaky Sub

Submarines can both float on the water and dive out of sight. So Phineas and Ferb build one to explore the ocean depths! But Candace catches onto their plan. She slips into the sub when the boys aren't looking. Let's see where Candace is heading.

Warning!
Have an adult help you with this experiment.

What You Need:

- Small plastic soda bottle
- Scissors
- 8 coins
- Tape
- Bendy straw
- Modeling clay
- Large bowl
- Water

What You Do:

1. Have an adult use scissors to poke a dime-sized hole halfway up the side of the plastic bottle.

2. Tape two stacks of four coins. Then tape one stack by the side of the hole near the bottom of the bottle. Tape the other stack by the side near the top of the bottle.

3. Set the bottle on the table so it rests on the coins. Stick the short end of the bendy straw into the mouth of the bottle. Angle the long end of the straw up. Seal the mouth of the bottle around the straw with clay. Make sure it is watertight.

4. Fill the bowl with water. Then place your submarine in the bowl with the straw sticking out of the water. Squeeze the bottle a couple of times to fill it with water.

5. Blow into the straw. The sub rises to the surface!

What's Happening Here?

A submarine pilot can control whether the ship sinks or floats with the help of **ballast tanks**. These tanks can be filled with water to make the ship heavier so it dives down. If the water in the tanks is pumped out and replaced with air, the ship rises. Your sub works in the same way, with you filling the tank!

Shell Shocker

Even at the beach, Dr. Doofenshmirtz is up to no good. He has set up a trap to stop Agent P from tailing him. Yikes! Agent P falls in. He's now stuck inside a giant clamshell! Will Agent P be able to break out of the shell and escape? Let's see!

What You Need:
- Small seashell
- Glass
- White vinegar

What You Do:
1. Put the shell in the glass.
2. Fill the glass with enough vinegar to cover the shell.
3. Let the glass sit for three days. Check on your shell each day and see if you notice any changes.
4. At the end of the three days, remove the shell from the vinegar. Press down on the shell. Whoa!

What's Happening Here?
The shell is no longer hard! Seashells are made of calcium carbonate. This **mineral** is also found in bones and teeth. It's what makes them so hard and strong. Vinegar is an acid that **dissolves** calcium carbonate. It breaks down the mineral into calcium, which sinks to the bottom of the glass. This process also releases bubbles of carbon dioxide. Dissolving the calcium carbonate leaves a soft shell. Agent P should have no problem escaping now!

This Week's Roundup

This week's beach vacation made a giant splash! Fill in the chart to keep track of the experiments you've completed.

EXPERIMENT		DESCRIBE THE RESULTS OF THE EXPERIMENT
15.	Castle Construction	
16.	Sink or Swim?	
17.	Ship Shape	
18.	Buried Treasure	
19.	Dive! Dive!	
20.	Sneaky Sub	
21.	Shell Shocker	

Now Try This!

Let's go on a treasure hunt. Find these 10 words hidden in the word-search puzzle:

Buoyancy   Beach

Sand   Water

Magnet   Dissolve

Scuba   Ballast

Atlantis   Mineral

B	U	O	Y	A	N	C	Y	O	E
K	L	D	I	S	S	O	L	V	E
B	E	A	C	H	R	A	T	E	P
A	G	O	R	M	U	I	N	S	M
L	P	M	W	A	T	E	R	D	I
L	B	U	C	G	P	T	Y	A	N
A	T	L	A	N	T	I	S	E	E
S	V	O	N	E	N	Y	R	A	R
T	H	U	B	T	R	N	P	S	A
L	O	S	C	U	B	A	E	I	L

Be sure to look horizontally, vertically, and diagonally.

Turn to page 136 to check your answers.

WEEK FOUR

Road Trip

HONK! HONK! The Flynn-Fletcher family has piled into their camper van for a cross-country road trip. Along the way, they'll visit historic sites and take lots of photos for the family scrapbook. Will Phineas and Ferb have to put their inventing on hold? No way! They've got a few ideas to pass the time, like bridging the Grand Canyon, driving a remote-controlled monster truck, and having a car chase. Buckle up and get ready to roll!

Speed Racer

The road trip has just gotten started. But being stuck in a car can be a little boring. It doesn't take long for Phineas to come up with a way to make the journey more exciting. He and Ferb are going to rev up the camper van's engine to give it more pep. Get ready to rock and roll!

What You Need:
- Spool
- Rubber band
- Paper clip
- Tape
- Washer
- Pencil

What You Do:

1. Hook one end of the rubber band onto the paper clip. Insert the other end of the rubber band through the hole in the center of the spool.

2. Tape the paper clip to the end of the spool.

3. Thread the other end of the rubber band through the washer.

4. Slide the pencil about 1.5 inches through the rubber band loop.

5. Hold the spool with one hand. With the other, wind the rubber band by turning the pencil away from you. Wind until it sits tightly against the spool.

6. Once you've wound up the racer, set it—with pencil and paper clip at the sides—on a flat surface. (A carpeted floor works best.) Let go. Watch it zip forward!

What's Happening Here?

Winding up the rubber band set your spool racer in motion. This takes energy. You might remember from page 23 that energy never disappears. The energy you use to turn the pencil transfers from your muscles to the rubber band. As the rubber band unwinds, that energy transforms into **mechanical energy**, rolling the spool forward.

Bridge the Gap

Phineas and Ferb are getting antsy on the road, so they devise a shortcut. But it requires crossing the Grand Canyon! No bridges span this huge gorge. The boys will have to build one. The bridge needs to be able to support lots of cars full of sightseers. That will take some clever construction so the bridge won't collapse. Try and work out how they'll do it.

What You Need:
- Index cards
- Books
- Pennies
- Pencils
- Tape
- String

What You Do:

1. Make two stacks of books that are the same height with 3 inches between the stacks.

2. Lay an index card lengthwise across the gap.

3. Pile pennies in the middle of the card. How many can it hold before collapsing?

4. Try making your index card bridge stronger by folding the card in half, in pleats, or in an arch. Try using the pencils, string, and tape to support the bridge.

5. Test your designs to see how many pennies they will hold.

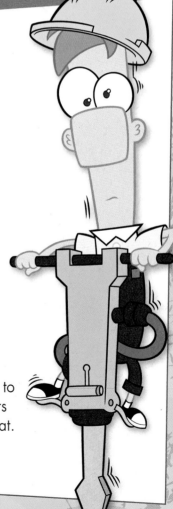

What's Happening Here?

The flat index card mimics the simplest form of a bridge—a straight beam across a gap. Adding a heavy **load** pushes down on the bridge. If the load is more than the bridge can handle, it will buckle. One way to make a bridge stronger is to spread the force of the load out over a larger area. Engineers use arches, **trusses**, and **suspension cables** to do just that. Did any of these elements make your bridge stronger?

Moldy Print

Ew! Candace smells something stinky in the camper van. She searches the car for the source of the smell. Under the seat she discovers a half-eaten sandwich, and it's covered in mold. YUCK! Could she use it as evidence to get her brothers in trouble? Let's find out.

What You Need:
- Slice of bread
- Paper towels
- Plate
- Sealable plastic bag

What You Do:

1. Use a paper towel to remove a slice of bread from its bag. Try not to touch the bread directly with your hands.

2. Set the bread on a plate.

3. Look for a dusty area in your home. Put one of your palms in the dust.

4. Place your dusty palm on the bread slice.

5. Using a paper towel again, pick up the bread and place it in your bag. Seal the bag.

6. Put the bag handprint side up in a dark place for a few days.

7. Take a look at your bread slice. Yucky mold!

What's Happening Here?

Dust contains mold **spores**. These microscopic particles travel in the air, and are all around you. When you stick your hand in the dust, you pick up some spores, transferring them onto the bread. Spores need the right conditions to grow. They thrive in moist, dark areas. They grow into a fuzzy fungi on your bread! The sandwich Candace found might have grown mold where someone touched it. Do you think she can match the moldy handprint to the culprit?

Car Chase

Agent P spots Dr. Doofenshmirtz zooming down the highway. Agent P ducks out of the camper van and lands in a secret-agent scooter. Let's watch the car chase!

What You Do:

1. Blow up the balloon and knot the end.
2. Rub the balloon on your hair.
3. Set the can on a flat surface. Hold the balloon about an inch away in front of the can. The can rolls toward the balloon!

What You Need:
- Balloon
- Empty soda can

What's Happening Here?

All things in the universe are made of tiny particles called **atoms**. In each atom are negatively charged particles called **electrons** and positively charged particles called **protons**. Most of the time, these charges are balanced in an object. But when you rub the balloon on your hair, the electrons from your hair build up on the balloon. This creates **static electricity**. The excess electrons in the balloon have the power to attract protons in different objects. This attraction causes the can to chase after the balloon.

Zoomed In

Phineas and Ferb arrive at Mount Rushmore. The giant faces of Presidents George Washington, Thomas Jefferson, Theodore Roosevelt, and Abraham Lincoln are carved into the mountain. The boys have an idea for how to get an up-close view.

What You Need:
- Paper clip
- Pencil
- Glass of water
- Old newspaper

What You Do:

1. Bend the paper clip so it is straight. Then bend one end around the shaft of a pencil to form a tightly closed loop.
2. Remove the loop from the pencil. Dip the loop into the glass of water.
3. Hold the loop (filled with a water droplet) in front of an old piece of newspaper you don't mind getting wet.
4. Look through the loop. The letters appear bigger! (You may need to adjust the distance of the loop between the paper and your eye until you get a clear view.)

What's Happening Here?

The curved water droplet in your magnifier acts like a **convex lens**. This type of lens is used in microscopes and magnifying glasses. Light rays bend as they pass through the lens. The rays' new angles make objects look like they are closer to your eye than they really are. Your magnifier will make letters appear about five times larger!

Remote-Controlled Vehicle

Candace is learning how to drive! This could be scary. So Phineas and Ferb build their sister a remote-controlled monster truck. This way, they can keep everyone on the road safe!

What You Need:

- 2x3-inch piece of cardboard
- 8x10-inch piece of cardboard
- Scissors
- 2 strong magnets
- Clear tape
- 2 straws
- Glue
- 4 round candies with holes in their centers
- Books

What's Happening Here?

All magnets have a north and a south pole. When you hold the same poles of two magnets together, they repel, or push each other away. But when you hold opposite poles together, they attract. If your bottom magnet is flipped to the right side, the car will move.

What You Do:

1. Tape a magnet to the center of the small piece of cardboard.

2. Cut the straws to make two pieces that are each 4 inches long.

3. On the side of the card with the magnet, glue the straws across the two short sides. An inch of straw should stick out on each side.

4. Thread a candy "wheel" through the ends of each straw.

5. Stack two sets of books so they are the same level. Use the large piece of cardboard to bridge the two stacks of books. Put the car—magnet side down—on the cardboard.

6. Move the other magnet along the underside of the cardboard bridge. Can you control the car?

Cool Caves

There's just one last stop on this camper-van adventure. The family is going to explore some caves before heading back to Danville. Deep underground, Phineas and Ferb see all sorts of weird rock formations. Hanging from the roof of the cave are dripping stalactites. Let's watch one grow!

What You Need:

- 2 small glass jars
- Warm water
- Baking soda
- Spoon
- 2 paper clips
- Foot-long piece of yarn
- Saucer

What You Do:

1. Fill both jars with warm water. Stir baking soda into each glass until no more dissolves.

2. Attach a paper clip to each end of the piece of yarn.

3. Set the jars on a table with the saucer in between.

4. Dip each end of the yarn into a jar so the rest of the yarn hangs between.

5. Let the jars sit for a few days. Don't touch them! Observe what grows!

What's Happening Here?

Like your experiment, real stalactites form from mineral-rich water! In nature, stalactites form in limestone caves. When water carrying minerals seeps through the rock to the roof of a cave, a chemical reaction occurs. A ring of minerals is left behind. Over centuries, these minerals accumulate into columns. If you examine your saucer, you might also find a column growing upward. In a real cave, water dripping off a stalactite can land on the cave floor. The water can leave behind minerals that cause **stalagmites** to grow upward.

This Week's Roundup

You did it! Seven more projects finished! Fill in the chart to keep track of the results of your experiments.

EXPERIMENT	DESCRIBE THE RESULTS OF THE EXPERIMENT
22. Speed Racer	
23. Bridge the Gap	
24. Moldy Print	
25. Car Chase	
26. Zoomed In	
27. Remote-Controlled Vehicle	
28. Cool Caves	

Now Try This!

Phineas and Ferb decided to snap some photos and put them into an album. The boys want to make their book extra special by writing funny captions to go with their pictures. Help them out!

WEEK FIVE

Cirque des Sciences

Phineas, Ferb, and their friends have been counting the days till the circus comes to town. But they just learned that the show has been cancelled. What now? The gang decides to put on their own circus! They invite the entire neighborhood to come and watch. Step right up and see high-flying acrobats, Perry dressed as a clown, and the magician Baljeet the Magnificent!

Takeoff!

Phineas, Ferb, and their friends are ready to show off their circus acts. Up first: Phineas and Ferb performing as acrobats. They'll use a catapult to launch themselves through the air. *Wheee!*

What You Need:

- Large tissue box
- Scissors
- 2 unsharpened pencils
- 2 rubber bands
- Plastic bottle cap
- Glue
- Paper clip
- Mini marshmallows
- Bowl

What You Do:

1. Have an adult use scissors to cut off the top of the box. Then on a long side of the box, at 2 inches from one end and half an inch down the top, cut a hole no wider than the shaft of your pencil. Make a matching hole on the opposite side of the box. Slide a pencil through both holes.

2. On the short side of the box opposite of the end with the pencil, have an adult poke a small hole close to the bottom center.

3. Glue the plastic cap to the top of the long side of the other pencil. (Let the glue dry!)

4. Cut a rubber band in half. Lay the second pencil across the pencil in the box. (Make sure this pencil doesn't touch either end of the box!) Wrap the strip of rubber band around where the pencils cross to tie them tightly together.

5. Cut the other rubber band in half. Loop it around the lower end of the top pencil. Thread the band's other end through the hole in the back of the box. Pull the rubber band until it is straight. Then knot it to a paper clip to hold the band in place.

6. Pull back the top end of the standing pencil. Set a marshmallow in the cap. Let go to fling the marshmallow! Try to land marshmallows in a nearby bowl.

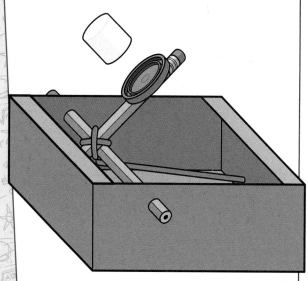

What's Happening Here?

Pulling back on the arm of your catapult stores a force called **tension** in the rubber band. Once you let go of the arm, the tension releases. This force whips the arm forward, launching your marshmallow. The marshmallow flies in an archlike path called a **trajectory**. The farther you pull back on the catapult's arm, the farther your marshmallow will fly.

Warning!
You need an adult helper
for this project.

Clowning Around

Look! It's Perry wearing a clown outfit. This disguise will help him stay undercover as he looks out for Dr. Doofenshmirtz. Perry just needs to practice some funny falls to blend in.

What You Need:

- Ping-Pong ball
- Scissors
- 6x2-inch piece of construction paper
- Tape
- Marble
- Marker

What You Do:

1. Have an adult use scissors to poke a small hole in the seam of a Ping-Pong ball. Then cut along the seam to split the ball in half.

2. Roll the construction paper into a 2-inch-tall tube. Place one end of the tube into the inside of half a ball. Tape the tube together. Then tape it to the ball.

3. Drop the marble into the tube. Then tape the other half of the ball to the top of the tube.

4. Draw a clown on the tube, with its head near one ball half and its feet near the other.

5. Place your clown on a slope and give it a gentle push. Tumble!

What's Happening Here?

If you set your clown tumbler on a flat surface, it stands upright. That's because the clown's **center of gravity** is in its base. But set your tumbler on a slope and it starts to flip. The marble rolls from one end of the tumbler to the other, causing the clown's center of gravity to move!

Balancing Act

Isabella is practicing her tightrope act. She has excellent balance—and even has a poise badge to prove it! Watch her!

What You Need:

- Metal spoon
- Metal fork
- Tall drinking glass
- Water
- Toothpick

What You Do:

1. Lace the tips of the fork and spoon together: Wedge the two outside prongs of the fork over the back of the spoon. Wedge the two inside prongs inside the bowl of the spoon.

2. Stick a toothpick through the fork's two center prongs where the utensils meet.

3. Set a glass on a flat surface. Fill it halfway full with water.

4. Set the toothpick on the edge of the glass. Adjust the toothpick until the fork and spoon balance on the glass.

What's Happening Here?

Like in the previous experiment, an object balances around its center of gravity. When you find this spot on the toothpick, the fork's and spoon's weights will be evenly spread! The toothpick is a **fulcrum**. If you touch the spoon or fork while it's balancing, you will cause it to rock around this pivot point.

Flying Orbs

Buford has a skill that will be perfect for the backyard circus. He can juggle five balls at once—while blindfolded! That's quite a feat! Here's a challenge: Try and keep just one ball in the air.

What You Do:

1. Bend the straw so that the short end crooks into a right angle.

2. Place the long end of the straw into your mouth. Turn the bended end so it is pointing upward.

3. Hold the Ping-Pong ball directly over the top of the end of the straw.

4. Blow a steady stream of air and let go of the ball. Try not to move too much. The ball floats above the straw!

What's Happening Here?

This trick works because of something called **air pressure**. You learned earlier that everything in the universe is made of atoms and **molecules**. Air, too, is made up of molecules. These air molecules are constantly pushing down on you. This is air pressure. When you blow through the straw, a stream of fast-moving air shoots up. This creates a pocket of low pressure around the ball. Because the air outside the pocket is slower moving, it has a higher pressure. The higher-pressure air forces the ball to stay inside the pocket. This causes the ball to suspend in the air. This experiment demonstrates something called **Bernoulli's principle**. It explains that as the speed of gas increases, the pressure it exerts decreases.

Trapeze Time

Candace talks Jeremy into performing on a flying trapeze. She wants him to dangle by his knees from a swing and catch her as she leaps into the air. They'll basically be holding hands! Candace is so excited. But she has to time her jump just right, otherwise she could send Jeremy swinging wildly. Let's practice this move.

Warning!
This project is messy. Cover your work area with newspaper.

What You Need:

- Two 1-yard-long pieces of string
- Two chairs
- Tape
- Black poster board
- Paper cup
- Salt
- Sharpened pencil

What's Happening Here?

When you release the trapeze in step five, you apply an outside force to it. This causes it to move. Because of the way the support string is set up, the trapeze travels steadily back and forth. But when you twist the trapeze before releasing it, it swings in a circle. That's because there's another force besides you acting on the trapeze. The new position causes the support string to swing freely forward and back. This tugs on the cup. The combination of the forces causes the cup to move left and right, as well as back and forth.

What You Do:

1. Place two chairs, with their backs facing each other, about a foot and a half apart. Tape one end of a piece of string to the top of each chair.

2. Place your poster board on the floor between the chairs.

3. Tape one end of your other piece of string to the rim of the paper cup. Loop the string over the one strung between the chairs. Then tape its other end to the opposite side of the cup. The cup should look like a hanging basket, and it shouldn't touch the ground.

4. Use the pencil to poke a small hole in the bottom of the cup. Use a piece of tape to cover the hole. Then fill the cup with salt.

5. Pull the cup toward a chair. Make sure the basket, or "trapeze," faces the other chair. Remove the tape and let go of the cup. Watch the pattern of salt!

6. When the trapeze makes it over to the other side, place a piece of tape over the hole in the cup. If needed, refill the cup with salt.

7. Twist the string so that the trapeze is turned away from the chair. Pull the cup toward the edge of the poster board. Remove the tape and let go. Whoa! Crazy moves!

Magic Trick

Baljeet joins the circus troupe and puts on a magic act. His stage name is Baljeet the Magnificent. What tricks does he have up his sleeve? First Baljeet will make two colors magically mix to form a new one. He won't give away the secret to this magic trick. Perform this experiment to figure it out.

What You Need:

- Two baby-food jars
- Warm water
- Cold water
- Yellow and blue food coloring
- Index card
- Large pan

Warning!
You need an adult helper for this project. Food coloring can stain.

What You Do:

1. Fill one jar to the rim with warm water. Fill the other with cold water.

2. Add two drops of blue food coloring to the cold water and two drops of yellow food coloring to the warm water.

3. Set the warm jar in the pan to catch any spills.

4. Place the index card over the mouth of the cold-water jar. Make sure to completely cover the opening.

5. Holding the card tightly in place, flip the cold-water jar upside down and set it on top of the warm-water jar. Line up the mouths of the jars.

6. Holding the top jar, carefully slide the card out. Abracadabra! The colors mix!

What's Happening Here?

After removing the index card, the blue and yellow water begin to move. The different temperatures of the water in the two jars cause **convection** to occur. The denser cold water sinks and the lighter warm water rises. As they mix, they form a new color—green! In the ocean, convection keeps the water in motion. Convection in the atmosphere stirs up the air, causing thunderstorms to form.

Flower Power

Baljeet the Magnificent has already pulled a rabbit out of his hat. For his final trick, he produces a white bouquet out of thin air and hands it to Isabella. Hold on! The flowers are changing color right before her eyes! Wow!

What You Need:

- 2 white carnations (You can use celery stalks if you can't find carnations.)
- Red and blue food coloring
- Water
- Two tall drinking glasses

Warning!
Food coloring can stain. Handle with care.

What You Do:

1. Remove any leaves from the carnations (or celery pieces) and snip half an inch off the bottom of the stem (or stalks).

2. Fill two glasses a third full of water. Add 20 drops of red food coloring to one glass and 20 drops of blue to the other.

3. Place one stem (or stalk) in the red glass and the other stem (or stalk) in the blue glass.

4. Leave the flowers (or celery stalks) overnight. What do they look like the next morning?

What's Happening Here?

Where does the water go when you water a plant? The plant's thirsty roots suck it up! Then **capillary action** carries the liquid up the plant's stem to its leaves and flowers. Inside a plant's stem are tiny tubes. Water molecules stick to one another and the sides of the tubes and slowly rise. By coloring the water, you can see this process in action. Once the water from each glass reaches the flowers, the petals become dyed red and blue. (For celery, the veins running up the stalks will be dyed.)

What a thrilling week! Let's fill in the chart to keep track of the experiments you've completed.

EXPERIMENT	DESCRIBE THE RESULTS OF THE EXPERIMENT
29. Takeoff!	
30. Clowning Around	
31. Balancing Act	
32. Flying Orbs	
33. Trapeze Time	
34. Magic Trick	
35. Flower Power	

Now Try This!

Agent P sure looks funny in his disguise. You know what's just as funny? Science jokes! See if they get a laugh out of a friend or family member. To find the punch lines, turn to page 136.

1. What dinosaur crushes everything in its path?

2. Why do tigers have stripes?

3. What works only when it's fired?

4. What kind of plates do astronauts use?

5. Why don't skeletons go skydiving?

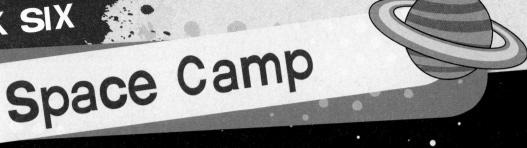

WEEK SIX

Space Camp

Phineas and Ferb are off to space camp! They're going to have an out-of-this-world time training to become space cadets! They've got their spacesuits ready and a map to navigate the Milky Way. Who knows what types of stellar adventures the pair will have? They might even launch a rocket, fly in a jet, and visit another planet! It's time to head for the stars!

Air Rocket

As the bus pulls into space camp, the first thing Phineas and Ferb see is an old rocket. Phineas immediately turns to Ferb and says, "I know what we're gonna do today!" He tells Ferb that they are going to use the rocket to launch their own space station into orbit! Get ready to 3 . . . 2 . . . 1 . . . liftoff!

What You Need:

- Pencil
- Paper
- Scissors
- Tape
- Plastic coffee stirrer
- Empty dishwashing liquid bottle (cleaned, dried, and cap removed)
- Straw

What You Do:

1. Use the pencil to draw a half circle on the paper. Cut it out and roll it into a cone with a small opening at the tip. Tape the cone to hold it together.

2. Stick the stirrer so it just peeks out of the hole at the tip of the cone. Tape the stirrer to the inside of the top of the cone to hold it in place. Cover the stirrer's top (rocket tip) with tape.

3. Place the straw in the dishwashing liquid bottle. Place your hand around the mouth of the bottle to hold the straw in place.

4. Cover as much of the mouth of the bottle as possible. You want your hand to make an airtight seal.

5. Slide the stirrer into the straw.

6. Point the bottle away from you. Give it a powerful squeeze. Your rocket lifts off!

Warning! This project has flying parts. Do it outdoors. Wear goggles to protect your eyes.

What's Happening Here?

By covering the top of the bottle with your hand, you trap air inside. Squeezing the bottle increases the air pressure inside the bottle. That forces the air molecules inside the bottle to move up the straw—the only way out of the bottle! As the air rushes out, it pushes against the cone of the rocket. This force launches your rocket! The coffee stirrer helps the cone fly in a straight line.

Mission to Mars

Phineas and Ferb are being trained for a future mission to Mars. Today they are strapped into a machine that mimics the experience of being blasted into space. Whoa! The boys are being tossed around and around. They are getting dizzy and starting to see things. Check out what they are seeing!

What You Need:

- Paper plate
- Whole or 2% milk
- Red, blue, and yellow food coloring
- Dishwashing liquid
- Cotton swab

Warning! Food coloring can stain. Handle with care.

What You Do:

1. Pour enough milk to cover the bottom of the paper plate.

2. Add a drop of red, blue, and yellow food coloring near the center of the plate.

3. Dip a cotton swab into dishwashing liquid.

4. Touch the swab to the center of the plate. WHOA! Check out the swirling colors!

What's Happening Here?

That's a dizzy display of swirls. Where does it come from? Milk is mostly water. But it also contains droplets of fat. These substances can't connect on their own. But they can connect with the dishwashing liquid. That's because dishwashing liquid contains **polar molecules**. Rapid connections make the milk move. As it moves, molecules of food coloring get bumped. The action stops once the dishwashing liquid is mixed evenly into the milk. Add another drop to restart the motion.

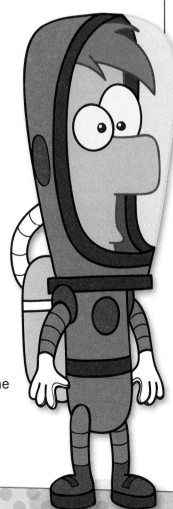

Hoop Glider

Everyone at space camp gets to practice flying in a flight simulator. Phineas and Ferb can't wait to test out their flying skills. Let's give this hoop glider a spin.

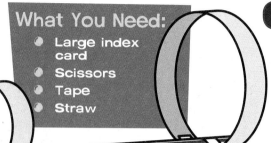

What You Need:

- Large index card
- Scissors
- Tape
- Straw

What You Do:

1. Cut the index card into three strips, each measuring 1 by 5 inches.
2. Curl one strip into a hoop and tape the ends together.
3. Tape the ends of the other two strips together to form one large hoop.
4. Thread the straw through the hoops. Then tape a hoop to each end of the straw.
5. Hold the glider by the middle of the straw. Have the hoops face upward and the smaller hoop face forward.
6. Throw your glider. Whee!

What's Happening Here?

Your glider doesn't resemble a plane, but it flew! The hoops may not look like wings, but they work the same way. They create lift. (You read about this on page 23.) The hoops also balance the straw so your glider flies evenly.

Balloon Jet

Jets can hit speeds of more than 2,000 miles per hour! Speed demons Phineas and Ferb are going for a ride with a trained pilot! They can't wait to zip through the air!

What You Need:

- 2 chairs
- Tape
- 3-yard-long piece of string
- Straw
- Balloon
- Paper clip

What You Do:

1. Space the two chairs 3 yards apart.
2. Thread the string through the straw. Then tape one end of the string to the back of each chair.
3. Drag the straw so it is next to one of the chairs.
4. Blow up the balloon. Use a paper clip to pinch the neck closed.
5. Tape the balloon to the straw with its neck pointed toward the closest chair. Remove the paper clip and let go of the balloon. *Whoosh!*

What's Happening Here?

The air rushing out of the balloon produces **thrust**. This force rockets the balloon forward. This is the same force that propels jet planes. Jets suck in air through the front of their engines. The air is heated, and then it's blasted out the back. The powerful jet of hot air propels the plane at superfast speeds.

Twirling Planet

Major Monogram reports that Dr. Doofenshmirtz is planning to steal Saturn's rings! Agent P teams up with Peter the Panda, another O.W.C.A. agent, to try to stop him. The duo uses a set of super thrusters to push the planet, causing it to spin faster. The spinning makes Dr. Doofenshmirtz too dizzy to carry out his plan. Let's give the planet a whirl.

What You Need:

- Paper
- Scissors
- Glue
- Sharpened pencil

What You Do:

1. Cut two strips of paper, each measuring 1.5 by 16 inches.

2. Lay the strips so they cross in the center. Here, glue the strip together. Allow the glue to dry.

3. Fold the four ends of the strips toward the center. Stack the ends on top of each other. Then glue the ends together. Let the glue dry.

4. Use a pencil to carefully poke a hole in the center of one set of overlapped strips. Do NOT poke through both sets. Push the pencil about 2 inches through the hole.

5. Hold the pencil between your palms and spin it quickly. Don't let go! Watch your "planet" spin!

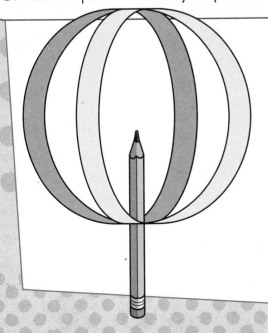

What's Happening Here?

Your planet, like the real ones in our solar system, spins and spins. All the planets orbit around the sun in a circular path. They also rotate on their own **axis**. Spinning around their center affects a planet's shape. As a planet spins, an apparent outward force causes it to flatten at the top and bottom and bulge at its center. Twirling the pencil mimics this motion and your paper planet bulges too. Spinning your planet faster will cause it to bulge even more. That will really make Dr. Doofenshmirtz dizzy!

Blast Off

Space camp is a blast! But Phineas and Ferb are ready to see space firsthand. They've designed their own spacecraft that will rocket them out of Earth's atmosphere. They just need to get the ship fueled up. Time to give these shooting stars a boost!

Warning!
This project has flying parts. Do it outdoors. Wear goggles to protect your eyes.

What You Need:

- Construction paper
- Scissors
- Tape
- Film canister (If you can't find one, try using a medicine bottle with a snap-on lid.)
- Spoon
- Cup
- 1 tablespoon baking soda
- 1/2 tablespoon water
- 1 tablespoon white vinegar

What You Do:

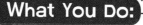

1. Cut the construction paper so it makes an 8-inch-tall tube that fits around the film canister.

2. Cut out four triangle "fins" from the paper. Also cut out a half circle to fold and tape into a "nose cone."

3. Tape the tube around the film canister with the lid on the bottom. Tape the fins so they stick out around the base of the tube. Tape the nose cone to the top.

4. In a cup, mix the baking soda and water. Pack the baking soda mixture into the canister's lid.

5. Tip your rocket upside down and pour the vinegar into the canister.

6. Quickly snap the lid onto the canister and place the rocket's base on a flat surface. Stand back. *WHOOSH!* Your spacecraft flies straight up!

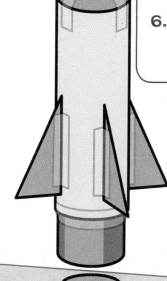

What's Happening Here?

When you combine baking soda and vinegar, a chemical reaction takes place. Vinegar is an acid and baking soda is a **base**. They react to produce carbon dioxide. The gas builds up inside the canister until the pressure is so strong the lid explodes off! The force of the lid flying one way pushes your spacecraft in the opposite direction.

Touch Down

Phineas and Ferb have made it to space, but they are running low on fuel. How will they get back to Earth? They've included an escape capsule that can detach from the spaceship. Once separated, a parachute shoots out of the capsule. Watch Phineas and Ferb as they drift safely back home!

What You Need:

- Plastic grocery bag
- Scissors
- Sharpened pencil
- String
- Washer
- Paper cup

Warning!
This project has flying parts. Do it outdoors. Wear goggles to protect your eyes.

What You Do:

1. Cut a large square from the grocery bag. Trim off the corners of the square to form an octagon.

2. Use the point of the pencil to poke a hole in each corner of the octagon.

3. Cut eight pieces of string, each a foot long. Tie a string to each hole. Then tie the ends of the strings to the washer.

4. Cut the paper cup in half. Keep only the bottom half. Poke a hole about a half inch from the top of the cup. Tie a 6-foot piece of string to the hole.

5. Place the washer in the cup. Next, tuck in the strings. Then ball up the parachute and gently pack it inside the cup.

6. Holding the long string, slowly swing the cup over your head. Increase your speed. Now tug the string sharply to toss the parachute high into the air. (This may take a few tries to get right!)

What's Happening Here?

When space flight first began in the 1960s, astronauts returned to Earth the same way! **Gravity** is the attractive force that pulls objects, including space capsules, toward the earth. Without a parachute, a capsule could be yanked down at dangerous speeds. A parachute has a large surface area. As it travels downward, its large surface snags a lot of air molecules. When air molecules push against the inside of the parachute, it creates a slowing force called **drag**. So the parachute—and anything attached to it—falls gently.

This Week's Roundup

Awesome! This week was out of this world. Fill in the chart to keep track of the results to your experiments.

EXPERIMENT	DESCRIBE THE RESULTS OF THE EXPERIMENT
36. Air Rocket	
37. Mission to Mars	
38. Hoop Glider	
39. Balloon Jet	
40. Twirling Planet	
41. Blast Off	
42. Touch Down	

Now Try This!

Phineas and Ferb spent a lot of time stargazing at space camp. They learned that constellations have Latin names. These names usually describe what the pattern of stars resemble. Below are some names of constellations, along with their English meaning in parentheses. Based on the information, can you match each picture of the constellations to its correct name? For answers to this puzzle, turn to page 136.

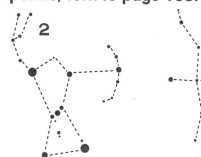
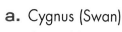
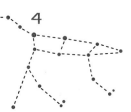

a. Cygnus (Swan)
b. Canis Major (Great dog)
c. Scorpius (Scorpion)
d. Orion (Orion, the hunter)
e. Ursa Major (Great bear)

WEEK SEVEN
Amusement Park

Danville is home to the biggest amusement park in the Tri-State Area! Guess what? Phineas and Ferb's parents give them two passes to check it out! Some of their friends are coming along, too. The boys are geared up for some thrills and spills. They're going to enjoy some tasty treats like cotton candy. Hopefully they'll be able to keep down their snacks when they take on the park's crazy rides. Let the fun begin!

Loop-de-Loop

The first ride Phineas and Ferb decide to go on is called the Looping Starship. It's a swinging ship that rocks back and forth. Then it swings in a complete circle, flipping riders upside down! Baljeet won't go on the ride until he can calculate what keeps the riders from falling out of their seats. Try this experiment to prove the ride is safe.

What You Need:

- Paper cup
- Scissors
- Two 3-foot-long pieces of string or yarn
- Water

What You Do:

1. Use the scissors to cut two small holes on either sides of the cup near the rim.
2. At each hole, tie a string to the cup.
3. Fill the cup about halfway full of water.
4. Hold both of the strings in one hand. Swing the cup fast so it makes a loop up and down. The cup flips over, but the water stays inside!

Warning!
This project can get messy. Do this outdoors.

What's Happening Here?

Mastering this project takes a little skill. But if you spin the cup smoothly and fast enough, you (and everything around you) won't get wet! When the cup reaches the top of the arc, gravity tries to pull the water out of the cup, making a mess. The **centripetal force** from the cup moving in a circle has to be greater than the force of gravity. Then the water will stay safely where it belongs—inside the cup!

De-Fizzer

All the soda in Danville has gone flat! Agent P suspects Dr. Doofenshmirtz, so he sneaks into Evil Incorporated. Agent P discovers a device that sucks the bubbles out of soda. Luckily, the machine has two switches. One is labeled "Remove Fizz," the other "Restore Fizz." Perry flips the "Restore Fizz" switch. Let's get the bubbles back!

What You Need:

- Glass jar
- 3/4 cups water
- 1/3 teaspoon salt
- Two paper clips
- Index card
- Aluminum foil
- C battery

Warning!

You need an adult helper for this project. Also, do NOT drink the results of the project.

What You Do:

1. Add the water to the jar. Stir in the salt.

2. Uncurl two paper clips so that there is just one hook left on each.

3. Poke the paper clips through the center of the index card about 1 inch apart.

4. Set the card on top of the jar with the hooks on top. The straight ends of the paper clips should be underwater. (If not, add more water.)

5. Cut two 4-inch-by-12-inch pieces of foil. Fold each in half lengthwise three times.

6. Wrap the end of one piece of foil around each paper clip's hook.

7. Touch the loose ends of the foil to the "+" and "-" ends of the battery. Look closely. The water is bubbling!

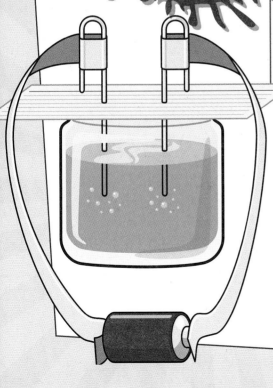

What's Happening Here?

A water molecule is made of two hydrogen atoms and an oxygen atom. That's why water is sometimes called H_2O! In this project, a process called **electrolysis** splits the water molecules into hydrogen and oxygen atoms. How? The foil and the paper clips are made of metal. Metals are good **conductors** of electricity. This allows electricity to travel from the battery into the water to break up its molecules. The bubbles you see are actually hydrogen and oxygen gas.

Take the Plunge

Phineas and Ferb are always up for a new thrill. So when they see a ride called the Tower of Terror, what do they do? They check it out! They climb in and strap themselves to the seats. Then the ride's speedy lifts pull the boys up, up, and up. At the top, the floor drops away. The riders' chairs plunge straight down! For a moment, the boys feel as if they are suspended in the air with their stomachs caught in their throat. Ahhh!

What You Need:
- Large index card
- Scissors
- Glass of water
- Penny
- Pencil

What You Do:

1. Cut two 1-inch-by-5-inch strips from the index card.

2. Tape the ends of the strips together to form a hoop.

3. Set the hoop upright in the mouth of the glass. Put the penny on top of the hoop.

4. Hold the pencil inside the hoop. Swing your hand so the pencil quickly flings the hoop away from you. The penny doesn't fly with the hoop; it nose-dives into the water instead!

What's Happening Here?

The penny doesn't fly away with the paper hoop. The reason is **inertia**. This is a tendency for objects to resist change in motion. When you fling the hoop, you act on the penny with an outside force. The penny resists moving with the hoop. But the strong force of gravity tugs it into the glass. How is this related to the flying feeling at the top of the ride? When traveling up the tower, the body moves up with it. When gravity suddenly pulls the ride down, the upward-moving body resists the sudden change in direction. For a moment, the body is still moving up while the ride is already yanking it down.

Screaming Spinner

Candace asks Jeremy to go to the amusement park with her. They decide to go on a ride that whirls and whirls around. Both Candace and Jeremy are calm until the ride starts up. Then Jeremy lets out an embarrassing high-pitched scream and grabs onto Candace. This is kind of what he sounded like!

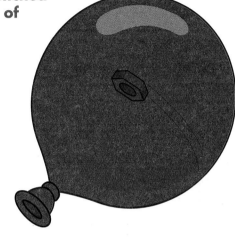

What You Need:
- Balloon
- Penny
- Hex nut (You can find this at a hardware store.)

What You Do:

1. Gently pull apart the mouth of the balloon and slide the penny inside. Be careful not to rip the balloon.

2. Blow up the balloon and tie it off. (Be careful. Only exhale into the balloon. Don't inhale or you might suck up the penny!)

3. With one hand, hold the balloon by its knotted opening. Then spin the balloon around. Now stop. The penny keeps whirling round and round the balloon!

4. Repeat the experiment with the hex nut instead of the penny. Not only does the hex nut spin, it screams!

What's Happening Here?

Just like the project on page 60, centripetal force is at work again! This force keeps the penny and hex nut moving in a circular path. Why does the penny whirl around without making a sound, while the hex nut shrieks like Jeremy? The penny has round edges and the hex nut has flat ones. Instead of rolling smoothly along the inside of the balloon, the hex nut's edges cause it to bounce around the balloon. This causes vibrations that travel to your ears as **sound waves**!

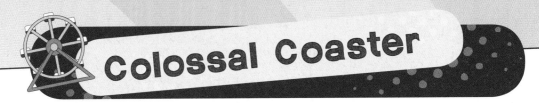

Colossal Coaster

This amusement park is home to the Beast, the biggest roller coaster in the Tri-State Area! The boys have been waiting in line for hours just for a chance to ride down this track. Phineas and Ferb decide that if they build their own roller coaster, they could ride it anytime. No more waiting in line! Let's help them design a coaster!

What You Need:
- Pieces of foam pipe insulation
- Scissors
- Tape
- Marble

What You Do:

1. Store-bought foam pipe insulation usually has a slit cut lengthwise. Cut the opposite side of the insulation so you have two long halves.

2. Connect the foam halves (cut side up) with tape to build your coaster track.

3. Time to build a track! Here are the rules:

   - The track must have any three of these elements: loops, corkscrews, turns, and hills.

   - You can use books, chairs, tables, tape, and other items to prop up or secure parts of your coaster.

   - In order for the track to be considered a success, the ball must be able to travel unassisted—and without stopping—from the beginning till the end.

4. Ready for a test run? Set a marble in the groove at the top of the track and let go. Did it make it through all the twists and turns? If not, adjust your track design and try again.

What's Happening Here?

The higher the first drop on your coaster is located, the more energy your marble will have to make it through your track's tricks. Starting at the top of the first hill, your marble builds up lots of potential energy. When you let go, gravity pulls the marble down. Its stored energy turns into kinetic energy. (You learned about these two types of energy on page 23.) The coaster needs a lot of moving energy to speed down the entire track.

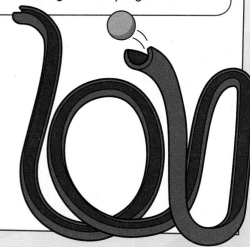

Defying Gravity

Phineas and Ferb want their coaster to do things no coaster has done before. It might even break some of the laws of physics like this experiment seems to do!

What You Need:

- Plastic jar equally wide at the top and the bottom
- Rubber bands
- Modeling clay
- Books
- Piece of cardboard

What's Happening Here?

The jar doesn't really defy gravity by rolling uphill. The key to its ability has to do with the jar's mass. An empty jar's mass is evenly placed around its center. The strip of clay shifts the jar's overall mass away from its center and to its side. You place the jar at the bottom of the hill so most of its mass is at the top. Gravity then pulls the mass downward, and the jar rolls forward up the ramp.

What You Do:

1. Wrap several rubber bands around the outside of the jar.
2. Roll a strip of clay as long as your jar. Press the clay along the jar's inside wall.
3. Build a ramp! Use books to prop up one end of a sturdy piece of cardboard. (You may need to adjust the ramp's height for this to work.)
4. Place your jar on its side at the bottom of the ramp with the clay on top. Rotate the jar a quarter turn toward the ramp. Now let go. The glass rolls uphill!

Flipping Out

Warning! This project is messy. Work over a sink.

The scariest ride in the park might just be the Zipper! As it goes round and round, its cars flip end over end over end. Isabella is willing to give it a go. Let's watch her flip out!

What You Need:

- Drinking glass
- Water
- Index card

What You Do:

1. Fill a glass as full as you can with water.
2. Place the index card on top of the glass. Make sure the card completely covers the rim of the glass.
3. Hold the card to the glass tightly and flip the glass over a sink.
4. Slowly let go of the card. Wow! The card stays in place; it sticks to the cup. The water doesn't spill!

What's Happening Here?

Isabella flipped around and didn't fall off! What made the index card stick? Air pressure outside the glass is greater than that inside the glass. That's because the glass is full of water; there is no air pressure inside! The air pressure outside the glass pushes the card upward, pressing it against the glass. This pressure is stronger than the weight of the water pushing down on the card. So the card sticks to the glass's rim.

What a super-fun week! Fill in the chart to keep track of the experiments you've completed.

EXPERIMENT	DESCRIBE THE RESULTS OF THE EXPERIMENT
43. Loop-de-Loop	
44. De-Fizzer	
45. Take the Plunge	
46. Screaming Spinner	
47. Colossal Coaster	
48. Defying Gravity	
49. Flipping Out	

Now Try This!

Let the fun continue! Complete this puzzle using the clues below. Hint: All the answers can all be found in this chapter. To find the answers, go to page 136.

Across

1. Centripetal _____ moves objects in a circular path.
2. Smallest possible particle of a chemical element
3. Thrill ride that uses a car to slide down a track
4. Soda that's lost its fizz
5. Amusement _____

Down

6. One of the types of atoms that make a molecule of water
7. Force that pulls objects toward Earth's surface
8. Aluminum is one type of this
9. Material that electricity or heat passes through easily
10. Ferocious animal

Stuck Indoors

Dr. Doofenshmirtz is out to ruin summer. He has built a weather-changing machine that pumps out storm clouds. Now it's raining cats and dogs across the Tri-State Area! Everyone is stuck indoors, waiting for the storm to blow over. Even though it's thundering outside, Phineas and Ferb are still determined to have fun. They find lots of ways to keep themselves busy indoors, including teasing Candace and throwing a party!

Ruined Artwork

The rain means Candace can't go out to see Jeremy. To pass the time, she decides to paint a portrait of him. She sets her finished painting by the front door to dry. Watch out! Perry comes in from outside and shakes his fur. That gets water all over Candace's artwork! Oops! Will the water ruin her painting by causing the colors to run? Let's find out.

What You Need:

- Black non-permanent marker (You can also use black watercolor paint.)
- Coffee filter
- Pencil
- Ruler
- Tape
- Glass
- Water

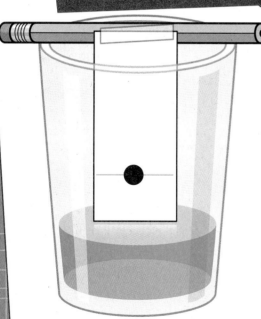

What You Do:

1. Cut a strip from your coffee filter. It should be 2 inches wide and 1 inch shorter than your glass.

2. At half an inch from the bottom of your filter strip, draw a line across using the pencil. On the line, draw a big black dot with the marker.

3. Tape the top of the filter strip to the pencil.

4. Fill the glass with slightly more than 1 inch of water.

5. Rest the pencil across the top of the glass so the strip hangs inside. It should just barely touch the water. Watch what happens. As the ink runs, hidden colors are revealed!

What's Happening Here?

Candace is not going to like this. Dyes used in markers and paints are actually made up of multiple colors. This project uses a process called **chromatography** to reveal the hidden hues. As the water creeps up the paper, it carries the dyes with it. Some inks travel farther than others, so the colors separate. How many colors were in the black dye?

Chatterbox

The gloominess outside has gotten to Phineas and Ferb. What they need is a good laugh. Playing a practical joke on Candace would be pretty funny. Hopefully Candace will feel the same way. She'll jump out of her skin when she hears a strange voice coming from the kitchen!

What You Need:

- Small plastic soda bottle
- Freezer
- Water
- Quarter
- Bowl

What You Do:

1. Put the empty bottle in a freezer and let it rest for 30 minutes.

2. Fill the bowl with water. Then dunk the quarter into the bowl.

3. When time's up, remove the bottle from the freezer. Immediately place the wet coin over the mouth of the bottle.

4. Gently place your hands on the bottle. The coin starts talking! Spooky!

What's Happening Here?

After being in the freezer, the air inside the bottle is very cold. The cold air molecules scrunch together. Your hands help warm up the air in the bottle. The warming air molecules start to spread out. Since the coin is sealing the bottle, the expanding air has to push past it to escape. That causes the coin to flutter up and down, making quite a racket!

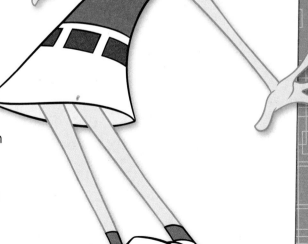

Hot House

It's still raining! Phineas and Ferb can't check on their plants outdoors, so they decide to bring the garden indoors. They build a greenhouse. Let's grow a new plant to put inside.

What You Need:
- Tall glass jar
- Dried beans
- Paper towels
- Water

What You Do:

1. Soak a dried bean in water for a day.

2. Wet several paper towels. Roll them up lengthwise and have them line the jar.

3. Slide the bean in between the glass and the paper towels. Put your jar in a warm place.

4. Put a little water in the jar each day to keep the paper moist. After a few days, your plant will begin to grow. Check out its progress through the glass.

5. Put your bean plant into a pot of soil to keep it growing.

What's Happening Here?

A bean is a seed of a bean plant. When a seed is buried in soil, it needs the right amount of moisture and heat for the seed to sprout. The glass jar provides the right conditions, allowing you to see what normally happens underground. Notice how the roots grow downward in search of water and the stem grows upward in search of light.

Plant Maze

It's a jungle inside the greenhouse! The boys better be careful, or they might get lost inside their maze of plants. See what's causing the plants to grow so wild.

What You Need:
- Shoe box
- Cardboard
- Scissors
- Clear tape
- Bean plant from the previous project

What You Do:

1. Cut two pieces of cardboard so they are as wide and deep as the short end of a shoe box.

2. Cut a window in each cardboard piece that takes up about half of one end.

3. Stand the shoe box on a short end. Cut a large window in the top.

4. Place your potted bean plant from the previous experiment inside the box.

5. Fit one cardboard piece into the box above your plant. Fit the other piece even higher up. The holes in the pieces should be on opposite sides. Use tape if needed to hold the pieces in place.

6. Put the lid on the box. Set the box in a sunny spot.

7. Every other day, remove the lid to water your plant and check on its progress. Did your plant make it through the maze?

What's Happening Here?

Plants can sense light and will always grow toward a sunny source. Why? They need light for **photosynthesis**. Plants use this process to harness sunlight and make food. That's why your plant bends to grow through the windows in the maze and out the top.

Lava Lamp

All of Phineas and Ferb's friends are stuck indoors, too. Why not invite everyone over for a party? Using their science know-how, the boys whip up some cool party decorations. Help them out by making a groovy lava lamp!

What You Need:

- Small plastic soda bottle (labels removed)
- Water
- Vegetable oil
- Red food coloring
- Fizzy antacid tablet

What You Do:

1. Fill the bottle one-fourth full of water.

2. Put four drops of red food coloring into the bottle.

3. Fill the bottle almost to the top with vegetable oil.

4. Break the antacid tablet in half. Drop it into the bottle. Check out the action!

Warning!
You need an adult helper for this project. You'll need to use an antacid tablet, which is a medicine. Do not eat! Food coloring can stain.

What's Happening Here?

The antacid tablet is the key ingredient to this super-groovy party! When it sinks below the oil and hits the water, it begins to fizz. This type of antacid contains an acid and a base. As the tablet dissolves, the acid and base react to produce bubbles of carbon dioxide gas. (The same reaction occurred in the experiment on page 56.) The bubbles rise to the surface, carrying blobs of red water with them. Once the bubbles burst, the water sinks beneath the oil again.

Let's Dance

Isabella, Baljeet, and Buford have all arrived for the party. Phineas and Ferb crank up the tunes. They can get just about anyone (or anything) to dance—even the items in their kitchen pantry!

What You Need:
- Plastic cup
- Plastic wrap
- Rubber band
- Rice
- Metal pan
- Wooden spoon

What You Do:

1. Stretch a piece of plastic wrap over the mouth of a cup. Wrap a rubber band around the cup's mouth to hold the plastic wrap in place.

2. Pull the edges of the plastic wrap down to stretch it as tightly as you can.

3. Put a few grains of rice on top of the plastic wrap.

4. Hold a metal saucepan near the cup and bang it with a wooden spoon. The rice dances around!

What's Happening Here?

Banging on the pan produces sound waves that travel through the air. When the sound waves reach the wrap, they cause the plastic to vibrate. You can see the vibrations because they cause the grains of rice to jump up and down. This rice really likes to boogie!

Wild Twister

Dr. Doofenshmirtz has set his weather-changing machine's dial to "stormy." But he accidentally bumps the device, turning it up to full power. That creates a tornado heading straight for downtown Danville! Agent P is on top of it! He manages to unplug the machine just in time and saves the day. See a twister in action.

What You Need:

- 2 small plastic soda bottles (labels removed)
- Water
- Food coloring
- Glitter
- Glue
- Washer
- Duct tape

What You Do:

1. Fill one bottle three-fourths full of water. Add five drops of food coloring and some glitter.

2. Dry off the bottle's opening and glue the washer on top. Turn the empty bottle upside down. Glue its opening to the top of the washer. Let the glue dry.

3. Tightly wrap duct tape around the necks of the bottles. They should make a watertight seal.

4. Above a sink, flip the bottles over and swirl the water in the top bottle.

5. If the bottles don't leak, set them on a flat surface. Spin, tornado, spin!

What's Happening Here?

Have you ever noticed how water swirls down the drain when you empty a sink or bathtub? As the water drains, a **vortex** forms. The same thing happens with your tornado in a bottle. As water flows out of the top bottle, air rushes up. A swirling hole forms in the center of the bottle! A real tornado's swirling winds pick up objects and pull them toward the center of the vortex. In your bottle, the vortex does the same, drawing the glitter toward the tornado's center.

This Week's Roundup

Well done! You stayed dried from the rain. Let's fill in the chart to keep track of the results of your experiments.

EXPERIMENT	DESCRIBE THE RESULTS OF THE EXPERIMENT
50. Ruined Artwork	
51. Chatterbox	
52. Hot House	
53. Plant Maze	
54. Lava Lamp	
55. Let's Dance	
56. Wild Twister	

Now Try This!

Phineas and Ferb need to water the plant in the center of this maze. Help them find their way! Turn to page 136 to find the solution.

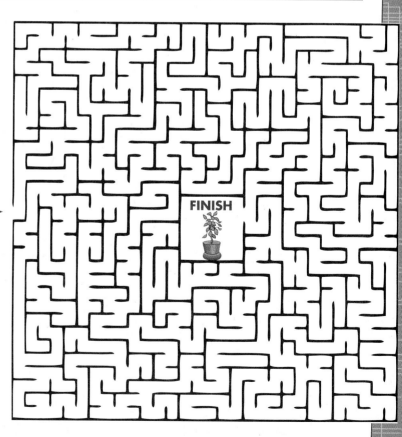

START

FINISH

WEEK NINE

European Vacation

It's time for a change of scenery. Phineas and Ferb are leaving the USA and heading overseas! Their first stop is England, the country where Ferb was born. The boys will tour the capital, London, in a hot-air balloon. Then it's on to France, where the boys use the famous Eiffel Tower to power one of their inventions. Look out, Europe, here they come!

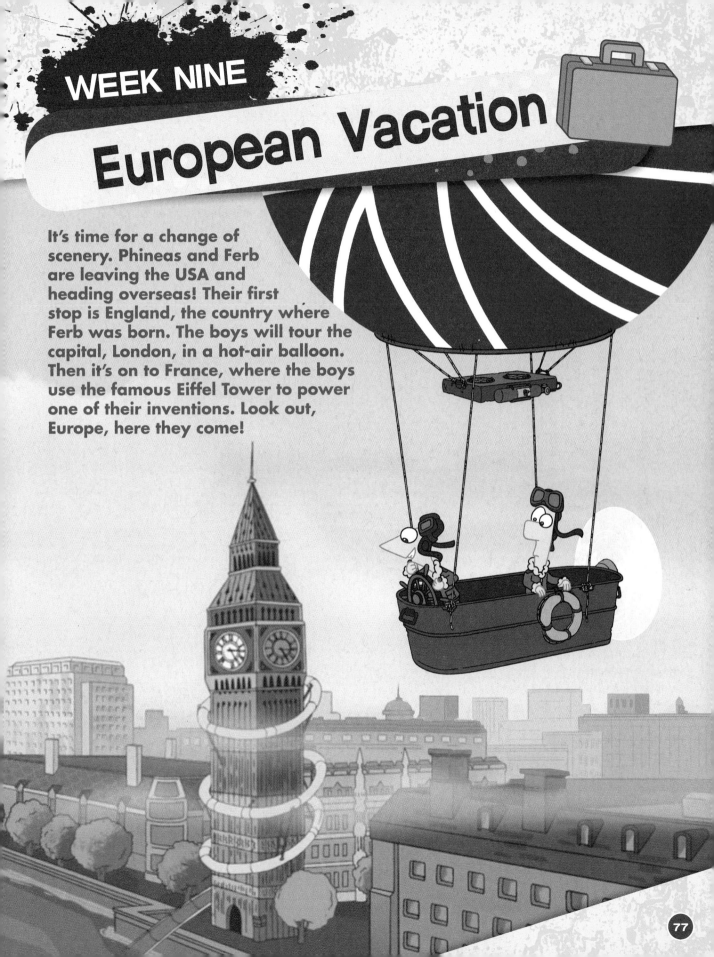

Balloon Blowup

Ferb's grandparents live in England, and the boys are stopping by for a visit. They can't wait to see London. With so much to see, Phineas and Ferb need a nifty way to catch all the city's sights. They build a high-tech balloon that instantly inflates!

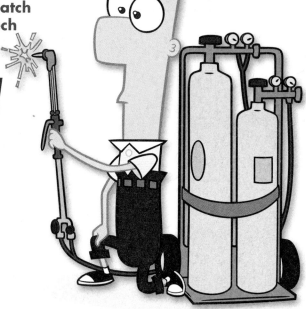

What You Need:

- Balloon
- 1/4 cup warm water
- 1 teaspoon of sugar
- Small plastic soda bottle
- Packet of yeast

What You Do:

1. Add the yeast, water, and sugar to the bottle. Swirl the bottle to mix.

2. Stretch the neck of the balloon over the mouth of the bottle.

3. Set the bottle in a warm spot for 20 minutes. The balloon blows up!

What's Happening Here?

A package of dried yeast is filled with **microbes**. Water brings the yeast back to life. When the tiny organisms wake up in your bottle, they get to work eating the sugar. They also produce waste in return—carbon-dioxide gas. The more gas the hungry yeast produce, the more your balloon fills and expands. No pump required!

Growing Goo

What You Need:

- Clean, disposable diaper
- Scissors
- Sieve
- Cup
- Waxed paper
- Water
- Salt

Phineas and Ferb have made a powder that makes anything grow to an enormous size. Oh no! Some of the powder accidentally got on Candace. Now she *really* is a big sister! The boys need to shrink her back to normal size before giant Candace tramples London! Let's see what happens.

What You Do:

1. Cut through the inside lining of the disposable diaper. Remove the stuffing from inside.

2. Place the stuffing in the sieve over a large piece of waxed paper. Gently shake the sieve and use your hand to mix up the stuffing. You'll see a white powder fall onto the waxed paper below.

3. Lift the waxed paper and carefully pour the powder into the cup.

4. Pour water into the cup and swirl. The powder expands! Turn the cup over. No water leaks out!

5. Now slowly stir some salt into the gel. The gel shrinks!

What's Happening Here?

Diapers are made to hold a lot of liquid. That's possible thanks to a superabsorbent powder inside the diaper. The powder is actually a polymer. You learned about these substances on page 22. The polymer latches on to water molecules, sucking them up like a sponge. The diaper dust can absorb more than 200 times its weight in water! As the water is slurped up, the polymer expands. It turns from a dry powder into a gooey gel. Adding salt breaks the bonds between the gel and the water and draws the liquid out of the gel.

Big Jumper

Big Ben is a giant clock tower in London. Phineas and Ferb want to check out the clock face, so they build a device that can bounce them up there. Can they do it? BOING! The duo flies to the top of Big Ben. Success! Let's see the jumper in action.

What You Need:
- Index card
- Scissors
- 12-inch ruler
- Tape
- Pencil (do not use one with a round shape)

What You Do:

1. Cut the index card in half lengthwise.

2. Tape one end of the paper strip to the end of the ruler.

3. Lay the ruler and the paper strip flat on the table. Then pull the untaped end of the strip toward the ruler. Curve the strip into an arch and tape the free end onto the ruler.

4. Place a pencil about 1 inch from the edge of a table. The length of the pencil should align with the table's edge.

5. Lay the ruler across the pencil so it balances. About 3 inches of the ruler should extend off the table.

6. Blow a steady stream of air over the card. When the ruler rises, stop blowing. (If nothing happens or if your ruler keeps rolling away, try rebalancing the ruler.) The ruler falls and does a backflip!

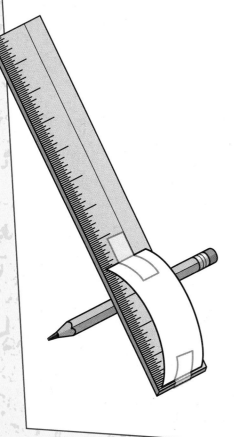

What's Happening Here?

Wings on a plane have a special design called an **airfoil**. This curved shape slices through the air as the plane moves and improves lift (remember this from page 23?). The card strip has a shape similar to an airfoil. Air blowing over the top of the card airfoil causes it to rise, lifting the ruler. Stop blowing and the ruler falls. If it hits the pencil with enough force, the ruler's opposite end springs up and over!

Spinning Top

One of the top attractions in London is a jumbo Ferris wheel called the London Eye. It takes 30 minutes for the giant wheel to make one turn. That gives riders lots of time to take in the sights. Phineas and Ferb decide that it would be much more fun if the wheel spun faster, so they soup it up. Now visitors are having an exciting time, but they are seeing London go by in a blur!

What You Need:

- Sharpened pencil
- White poster board
- Scissors
- Colored markers or paint

What You Do:

1. Cut out a 6-inch-wide circle from the poster board.

2. Draw lines on the circle to divide it into seven slices. Color one slice red, followed by slices in this order: orange, yellow, green, blue, indigo, and purple. (To make indigo, color its section purple. Then color over it with blue.)

3. Poke a pencil down through the center of the circle. About an inch of the sharpened end should poke through. (Note: The circle in the picture is flipped to show you the colors.)

4. Place the sharpened end of the pencil on a flat surface. Hold the eraser end of the pencil and give this top a spin. Try spinning the top slowly and quickly.

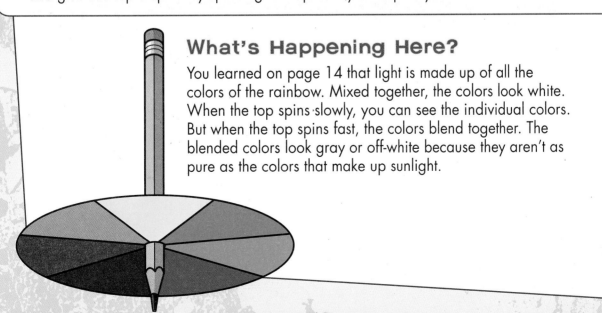

What's Happening Here?

You learned on page 14 that light is made up of all the colors of the rainbow. Mixed together, the colors look white. When the top spins slowly, you can see the individual colors. But when the top spins fast, the colors blend together. The blended colors look gray or off-white because they aren't as pure as the colors that make up sunlight.

Ready, Set, Charge!

Grab the suitcases and passports! It's time to cross the English Channel to visit Paris, France. Phineas and Ferb plan to use Paris's most well-known structure—the Eiffel Tower—as a lightning rod! When lightning strikes the metal tower, the boys plan to harness the electricity from the bolts to power their latest invention. To know when lightning might strike next, Phineas and Ferb build an electricity detector.

Warning!
You need an adult helper for this project.

What You Need:

- Glass jar
- Index card
- Scissors
- Nail
- 6-inch-long piece of thread
- Tape
- Aluminum foil
- Balloon

What You Do:

1. Cut a circle out of the index card. It needs to be large enough to cover the mouth of the jar. Push the nail about two-thirds through the circle's center.

2. Tie the middle of the thread to the pointy end of the nail.

3. Cut two small strips of foil and tape them to the ends of the thread.

4. Set the circle on top of the jar with the thread hanging inside. Tape the circle in place.

5. Blow up the balloon and rub it on your hair.

6. Touch the balloon to the top of the nail. The foil strips inside the jar move apart!

7. Touch the nail with your hand. The foil strips move back together!

What's Happening Here?

The device you made is called an **electroscope**. It detects an electrical charge, like the static electricity built up on the balloon. (You read about how rubbing your hair with a balloon builds static electricity on page 39.) When you touch the balloon to the nail, the charge travels down to the foil strips. Both strips become negatively charged. Since like charges repel against each other, the strips move apart. You absorb the charge when you touch the nail, so the foil strips collapse back together.

Money Exchange

Dr. Doofenshmirtz is causing trouble in Europe! What's he up to? He's changing tourists' loose change into funny-looking metal! People won't recognize the coins and will throw them away. Dr. Doofenshmirtz plans to collect the tossed coins and restore them to their original condition. Psst . . . here's the secret to his get-rich-quick scheme.

What You Need:

- 1 teaspoon of salt
- 1/4 cup vinegar
- Plastic bowl
- 10 dirty pennies
- Paper towel

What You Do:

1. Mix the salt and vinegar in a bowl. Add the pennies.

2. Let the pennies sit for five minutes, and then remove them. The pennies are shiny and clean! (Don't throw away your cleaning liquid yet. Save it for the next project.)

3. Rinse half of your pennies with water. Don't rinse the other half. Let the pennies sit on a paper towel for a few hours. Some of the pennies turned green!

What's Happening Here?

Vinegar is an acid. It reacts with the metal copper in the pennies. The vinegar at first cleans off the pennies' coating of tarnish, leaving them shiny. But if you don't rinse off the vinegar solution, blue-green **verdigris** appears. It forms as the acid reacts with the copper, the air, and the salt in the solution.

Copper-Coated

Agent P is onto Dr. Doofenshmirtz. He alerts Europe's banks about the disguised coins. But Dr. Doofenshmirtz has another idea. He's going to suck the precious metals out of the coins. Then he'll use the metals to make a copper statue of himself and put it in the middle of Paris!

What You Need:

- Penny-cleaning liquid from the previous project
- Paper clip
- Bowl

What You Do:

1. Place a paper clip in the bowl of penny-cleaning solution.

2. Let it sit for a few hours. Wow!

What's Happening Here?

Your paper clip changed from silver to copper colored! In the previous experiment, some positively charged copper **ions** dissolved in the solution while you were cleaning your pennies. Paper clips are made mostly of iron. When you place them in the solution, the acid dissolves some iron, too. That leaves a negative charge on the paper clip. Positive and negative charges attract. The copper ions stick to the paper clip's surface, giving it a copper coating.

This Week's Roundup

The week's over! You collected a lot of new stamps on your passport! To celebrate, fill in the chart to keep track of the experiments you've completed.

EXPERIMENT	DESCRIBE THE RESULTS OF THE EXPERIMENT
57. Balloon Blowup	
58. Growing Goo	
59. Big Jumper	
60. Spinning Top	
61. Ready, Set, Charge!	
62. Money Exchange	
63. Copper-Coated	

Now Try This!

See if you can unscramble the words below. All the jumbled words can be found in this chapter. For answers to this puzzle, go to page 136.

1. LDOONN _ _ _ _ _ _

2. LOABLON _ _ _ _ _ _ _

3. ROMICEB _ _ _ _ _ _ _

4. NGIHILTGN _ _ _ _ _ _ _ _ _

5. NPNEY _ _ _ _ _

6. FEELIF WROTE _ _ _ _ _ _ _ _ _ _ _

Unscramble all the highlighted letters above to answer the top secret question below.

The Secret Question:

What is Ferb's grandfather's name? _ _ _ _ _ _ _ _ _

Camping Out

The gang is spending the week at camp! They can't wait to go swimming, kayaking, and tell spooky campfire stories! Do Phineas, Ferb, and their friends have what it takes to tackle the great outdoors? Of course they do! Baljeet has made a list of the gear they'll need. Buford's ready to chop some firewood. And Isabella is a seasoned Fireside Girl. Looks like these campers are good to go!

Find Your Way

Isabella wants to earn her camping accomplishment patch. To do that, she needs to trek through the woods and find her way back to the campsite—all by herself! The only thing she can use to help her find her way is a compass. Let's make one!

What You Need:
- Waxed paper
- Scissors
- Magnet
- Sewing needle
- Clear tape
- Bowl of water

Warning!
Have an adult help you with this activity. It involves using a sharp object.

What You Do:

1. Cut a circle out of the waxed paper large enough to hold the needle.

2. Use the magnet to stroke the needle from the eye to the point 50 times. (Do not reverse direction. If you do so, your experiment will not work!)

3. Tape the needle to the paper.

4. Carefully float the waxed paper on the bowl of water. The needle will rotate until it is aligned to the North and South Poles. You've made a compass!

What's Happening Here?

Isabella will have no trouble finding her way. Earth has a magnetic field. It has a North and South Pole just like a magnet (see page 40). Rubbing the needle transfers some of the magnet's magnetic field to the needle. Floating the compass on water allows the needle to turn in different directions. It aligns with Earth's magnetic field, with one end pointing toward Earth's North Pole and one pointing toward its South Pole.

Spooky Sounds

Warning! You need an adult helper for this project.

By the time the gang has pitched their tents and set up camp, the sun has set. There's nothing left to do but sit around the campfire, roast marshmallows, and tell ghost stories. Phineas has the perfect spooky tale. It's sure to give his fellow campers a fright, especially when Ferb is making creepy sound effects. *EEK!*

What You Need:

- Large plastic cup
- Scissors
- 2-foot-long piece of string
- Water

What You Do:

1. Have an adult poke a hole in the bottom of the cup with the scissors. The hole should be just large enough for the string to fit through.

2. Tie a knot on one end of the string. Thread the other end through the mouth of the cup and out the hole. The knot should not pass through the hole.

3. Wet the string.

4. Hold the cup in one hand. Pinch the string with the thumb and forefinger of your other hand. Squeeze and slide your fingers down the string. It may take some practice. You'll know when you get it right because you'll hear a screeching sound!

What's Happening Here?

Your fingers both stick and slide as they move down the string. This causes the string to vibrate. The vibrations travel up the string and into the cup. Remember from page 73 that vibrations can be heard as sound waves. The hollow cup **amplifies** the sound so what you hear is a bone-chilling scream!

Buzz Off

BZZZ! The campsite is swarming with mosquitoes. The bugs are really starting to annoy the campers. Ferb has a plan. He whips up a supercharged bug zapper. Let's help him test out the *ZAP!*

What You Need:

- Styrofoam tray (like the ones that hold food from the supermarket)
- Scissors
- Aluminum pie tin
- Tape

What You Do:

1. Cut an L-shaped section off the edge of the Styrofoam tray. Gently bend the Styrofoam piece so it forms an arch.

2. Set the arch so it points up. Tape the ends to the pie tin like in the picture below. Your pie tin now has something that looks like a handle.

3. Rub the bottom of what remains of the Styrofoam tray against your hair for a few minutes. Set the tray upside down on a table.

4. Pick up the pie tin using the Styrofoam handle. (Don't touch the tin itself!) Hold the tin a foot over the Styrofoam tray and let go.

5. Now touch the pie tin. You feel a ZAP!

6. Try this experiment again. But before you touch the tin, turn out the lights. You'll see a spark in the dark!

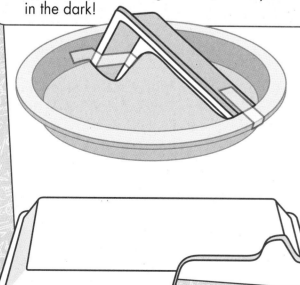

What's Happening Here?

Rubbing the tray on your hair builds up a static charge—a type of electricity (see page 39). When the metal pie tin touches the tray, the electricity jumps from the tray to the tin. The same thing happens when you touch the tray. The electricity jumps to your hand. That's the small zap you feel. You can even see the jolt of static electricity when you turn off the lights! SHOCKING!

Gone Fishing

The campers are going fishing. Oops, the camp counselors forgot to bring the fishing rods. Phineas gets an idea after seeing Buford tie Baljeet's shoelaces together. They can use shoestrings to reel in their lunch!

What You Need:
- Drinking glass
- Water
- Ice cube
- String
- Salt

What You Do:
1. Fill the glass nearly to the top with water. Put the ice cube in the glass.
2. Lay a string across the floating ice cube.
3. Sprinkle the top of the ice with salt.
4. Wait a few seconds and pick up the string. You caught an ice cube!

What's Happening Here?

Salt lowers the freezing point of water. This causes the ice to melt more quickly at room temperature. The string absorbs some of the water from the melted ice. The ice cube is still cold, though, so the water in the string refreezes. The result: The string is frozen to the ice cube. That's why you can lift up the ice.

Wild Water

Warning! This project is messy. Work over a sink.

Time to ride some raging rapids! Phineas, Ferb, and their friends have got their life jackets ready. But watch out! The river has churning water. Check out how these campers have found a way to go with the flow.

What You Need:
- 2 plastic cups
- 2-foot-long string
- Tape
- Water

What You Do:
1. Tape one end of the string to the inside bottom of each cup.
2. Fill a cup with water. Hold the cup above and off to the side of the empty one so the string is stretched tight. (Don't pull too hard or the tape will come unstuck!)
3. Tip the top cup and slowly pour the water down the string. It may take a few seconds, but the water will start to fill up the bottom cup!

What's Happening Here?

Water molecules like to stick together. This property is called **cohesion**. They also like to stick to other materials, like the string. This is called **adhesion**. When you pour water out of the top cup, gravity pulls the water downward. But instead of spilling everywhere, the water molecules hang on to the string and slowly travel together to the bottom cup.

Slimy Monster

Phineas and Ferb are hoping to catch a glimpse of the famous Lake Nose Monster. Many people have said they've seen the mysterious creature lurking in the lake. But no one has ever caught "Nosey" on camera. Hey, something slimy seems to be rising out of the water! Check it out!

What You Need:
- 1 cup cornstarch
- 1/2 cup water
- Food coloring
- Bowl

What You Do:

1. Use your hands to mix the cornstarch, water, and a few drops of food coloring in the bowl.

2. Scoop up a handful of slime. Feel it ooze through your fingers!

3. Dump the goop back in the bowl. Slowly push your fingers into it. They sink!

4. Slap the surface of the slime. Now it feels hard, not gooey!

Warning!
This project is messy. Food coloring can stain. Cover your work area with newspaper before you begin.

What's Happening Here?

It's not the monster, but it sure feels as weird and slimy as one. This slime is not a solid or a liquid; it's both! This slime is a type of material called a **non-Newtonian fluid**. Let the cornstarch mixture slowly run through your fingers, and it flows like a liquid. But when you quickly slap the mixture, the particles bind together and form a solid.

Invisible Perry

Now you see it, now you don't! Phineas and Ferb have built an invisibility beam. One zap can make any object disappear. A second zap can make the object return. Agent P borrows the invention to turn himself invisible. Now he can follow Dr. Doofenshmirtz without being seen. Let's make something else disappear!

What You Need:
- Quarter
- Clear drinking glass
- Water

What You Do:

1. Put the quarter on a table.

2. Set the glass on top of the coin. Look through the side of the glass. You can see the coin under the bottom of the glass.

3. Fill the glass with water.

4. Repeat step 2. What do you see this time? The coin disappears!

What's Happening Here?

What a disappearing act! You can see the coin under the empty glass because light rays bouncing off the object pass straight through air inside the glass. But pouring water into the glass changes things. The molecules in water are much closer together than those in air. This causes the light rays bouncing off the coin to refract, or bend. (You learned about refraction on page 14). The light never makes it to your eyes so the coin seems to vanish!

This Week's Roundup

Yay! You've finished another week of projects! Fill in the chart to keep track of the results to experiments.

	EXPERIMENT	DESCRIBE THE RESULTS OF THE EXPERIMENT
64.	Find Your Way	
65.	Spooky Sounds	
66.	Buzz Off	
67.	Gone Fishing	
68.	Wild Water	
69.	Slimy Monster	
70.	Invisible Perry	

Now Try This!

Write home about your camping trip! Below is a partially completed letter to help get you started. Just fill in the blanks with your own words!

Dear _____,
    person's name

We are having a(n) _____ time at camp. There are lots of _____ here to
           adjective   *noun (plural)*

keep us busy.

Phineas and Ferb told a great campfire story about a(n) _____ _____, while we
                                                            adjective *noun (singular)*

were roasting _____. Yesterday we went _____. The _____ were
         noun (plural)   *verb (ending in "ing")*   *noun (plural)*

really _____. Tomorrow we are going _____.
    verb (ending in "ing")   *verb (ending in "ing")*

You won't believe it but we saw a _____ in the lake! It was covered in _____!
                             noun (singular)   *noun (singular)*

Sleeping in a tent is loads of fun. Thanks to Baljeet, we packed plenty of _____. But I
                                                                   noun (plural)

may need more batteries for my _____. See you soon!
                           noun (singular)

_____
[Your Name]

Museum Volunteers

Guess who snagged summer jobs? Phineas and Ferb! They are helping out at the Danville Museum of Natural History. They are going to give tours, help at the snack bar, and work on building some new exhibits. This place has everything: fossils, a huge *T rex* skeleton, and mummies! The boys find even more weird science stuff hidden in the museum's creepy basement. Beware: This basement is haunted!

Fossil Footprint

There's a dusty box in a storeroom at the museum. What's inside? It's a fossil of a giant dinosaur footprint. Awesome! It gives Phineas an idea for a machine that could bring dinosaurs back to life. Until he manages that, the next best thing to real dinos is their crazy-big bones and prints. Let's get busy and make a fossil.

What You Need:

- 1 cup used coffee grounds
- 1/2 cup cold coffee
- 1 cup flour
- 1/2 cup salt
- Waxed paper
- Bowl
- Shells or other small, hard objects to "fossilize"

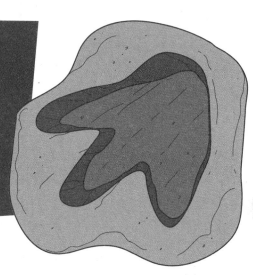

What You Do:

1. Mix the coffee grounds, cold coffee, flour, and salt in the bowl. Use your hands to squish the ingredients together.

2. Flatten out the dough on a piece of waxed paper.

3. Divide the dough into large squares.

4. Press a shell or other objects into the dough. Remove the objects to make imprints.

5. Allow your "fossils" to sit on the waxed paper for a few days. They will dry and harden.

What's Happening Here?

The prints you made look just like real fossils! **Fossils** are the preserved remains of living things from the past. They form when a plant or animal dies and is quickly buried by **sediment**. The soft parts of the animal rot away. Minerals seep into the animal's remaining bones, shells, or teeth. The minerals harden to form a fossil. Fossils can also be impressions of a plant or an animal's body part left behind in sediment.

Ghost Hunters

While mapping out a tour route for visitors, Phineas and Ferb stumble on a door to the museum's dark basement. Ferb thinks the basement is haunted, so they go in to search for a ghost.

What You Need:
- Tissue paper
- Scissors
- Balloon

What You Do:

1. Cut a ghost shape out of the tissue paper. It should be about 3 inches tall.

2. Blow up the balloon and knot the end. Rub the balloon on your hair.

3. Set the ghost on a table. Hold the balloon a few inches above the cutout. Whoa!

What's Happening Here?

The ghost floats off the table! On page 39, you learned that rubbing a balloon on your hair creates static electricity that can attract other objects. That's why the ghost stands up. If you make a super-tiny ghost out of tissue paper, it will completely jump off the table and fly up to the balloon. BOO!

Haunted Balloons

Things are looking creepy. The boys see items move by themselves! Could it really be a ghost? Let's see.

What You Need:
- 2 balloons
- 2 chairs
- Ruler
- String
- Straw
- Scissors

What You Do:

1. Blow up two balloons so they are the same size.

2. Put two chairs back to back slightly apart. Place a ruler so each end rests on a chair's back.

3. Tie a string to the neck of each balloon. Tie the other end of the strings to the ruler. The balloons should be even with each other with some space in between.

4. Use the straw to blow a steady stream of air between the balloons. The balloons don't move apart. Instead they move together!

What's Happening Here?

It's not a ghost. Just like on page 46, the motion is thanks to Bernoulli's principle. The faster the air moves, the lower the air pressure. Blowing between the balloons causes the pressure between the balloons to drop. Air moves from an area of high pressure to an area of low pressure. That sucks the balloons toward each other.

It's Alive!

One of Phineas's favorite places in the museum is the Egyptian Hall. It's filled with artifacts from ancient Egypt. There are lots of cool and creepy mummies that are thousands of years old. Ferb always imagines one might come to life, like in a monster movie. Want to see a mummy? Then try this.

What You Need:

- 1/3 cup salt
- 2/3 cup baking soda
- Bowl
- Apple slice

What You Do:

1. Mix the salt and baking soda in the bowl.

2. Put the apple slice into the bowl. Make sure it is completely covered by the salt mixture.

3. Set the bowl in a place that is cool, dry, and dark for a week.

4. Time's up! When you uncover your apple, it will be mummified!

What's Happening Here?

Ancient Egyptians made mummies to preserve people's bodies. First they removed all the organs. *EEWW!* Then they completely covered the body in a type of salt to dry it out. The salt sucks all the moisture out of the body so it won't rot. The same thing happens when you cover the apple slice with salt. Finally, Egyptians wrapped the preserved body in strips of cloth. This **desiccation** process worked so well, mummies still remain after thousands of years!

Iceberg Slicer

The museum is opening a new exhibit on icebergs. Phineas and Ferb are helping out by making some ice sculptures! The boys use a laser to cut through a large block of ice, shaping it to look like a rubber duck! Even though Phineas and Ferb cut through ice with a laser, it's possible to cut through ice with nothing but a fishing line!

What You Need:

- Metal fork
- Masking tape
- Heavy textbook
- Piece of fishing line
- Small plastic bottle of water
- Ice cube
- Aluminum foil
- Plate

What's Happening Here?

The weight of the bottle puts pressure on the fishing line. The pressure causes the ice to melt underneath the line. As the line slowly cuts through the cube, the melted water above it refreezes. By the time the line has cut through the entire cube, the ice still looks whole! What a cool trick!

What You Do:

1. Tape the handle of the fork to a table so the pronged end sticks out over the table. Place a heavy book on the handle.

2. Tie the fishing line around the neck of the bottle. Tie the line to make a 4-inch-wide loop that sticks out from the neck of the bottle.

3. Place the loop over the prongs of the fork. Can the fork support its weight? If not, add more books until it can, and remove the bottle from the fork.

4. Place an ice cube on a small square of foil on the fork. Set a plate on the floor under the fork. This helps catch any drips.

5. Loop the fishing line over the ice cube so the water bottle dangles just like when it was hanging from the fork.

6. Wait for the fishing line to move through the ice—without splitting the cube into two!

Rockin' Crystals

Candace finds a weird rock, so she has her brothers bring it to the museum for a scientist to examine. But on the way there, Ferb accidentally drops the rock and it cracks open. Oops. But wait! The boys discover that the rock is filled with sparkling crystals. Ooh . . . let's take a look at the pretty rock.

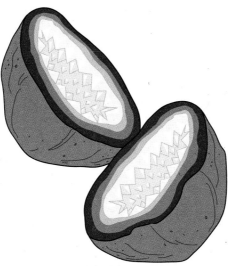

What You Need:
- Egg
- Spoon
- Bowl
- Epsom salts
- Food coloring
- 1/4 cup warm water
- Egg carton

Warning!
You need an adult helper for this project.

What You Do:

1. Have an adult crack the side of an egg with a spoon to break in half. Dump out the egg yolk and white. (You won't need this part of the egg, but an adult might want to save it for cooking.)

2. Rinse out the shell and remove the membrane inside.

3. Fill the bowl with warm water and a drop of food coloring. Stir in the Epsom salts until no more salt can dissolve.

4. Fill your eggshell with the mixture. Put the shell in the egg carton and set it in a sunny spot. Let it sit until all the water has evaporated. Wow! Check out the pretty crystals!

What's Happening Here?

Candace's rock is a **geode**! This type of rock forms when a hollow space inside a rock fills with water that contains dissolved minerals. As the water evaporates, it leaves the minerals behind. These minerals grow into **crystals**. The slower the water evaporates, the larger the crystals will grow. The same thing happens in your egg geode. It's lined with salt crystals!

Bouncy Quicksand

The museum is holding a water science event at Danville's public swimming pool. But Dr. Doofenshmirtz has replaced the water with quicksand! Luckily, something went wrong with Dr. Doofenshmirtz's quicksand formula. Instead of sinking, kids jumping into the pool bounce instead! YAY!

What You Need:

- 1/2 teaspoon Epsom salts
- 1/2 teaspoon warm water
- 2 bowls
- 1 tablespoon white glue
- Spoon
- Waxed paper

Warning! This project can get messy. Cover your work area with newspaper.

What You Do:

1. Mix the Epsom salts and water in a bowl until most of the salt dissolves.

2. Pour the salt mixture into another bowl. (Leave as much salt crystals behind in the first bowl as possible.)

3. Add the glue to the salt mixture in the second bowl and stir. A puttylike material starts to form.

4. Pull out the putty and set it on some waxed paper. Experiment with the putty. Does it stretch or bounce? Is it hard or soft?

What's Happening Here?

Glue is a type of liquid polymer. You learned about polymers on page 22. The polymer molecules in glue aren't bound together, so the glue flows. But a chemical in Epsom salts causes the glue molecules to connect. The glue becomes stretchy and less sticky. The new puttylike substance is called an **elastomer**. It's soft, flexible, and bouncy.

This Week's Roundup

Keep up the good work! You're sailing through these projects! Fill in the chart to keep track of the experiments you've completed.

	EXPERIMENT	DESCRIBE THE RESULTS OF THE EXPERIMENT
71.	Fossil Footprint	
72.	Ghost Hunters	
73.	Haunted Balloons	
74.	It's Alive!	
75.	Iceberg Slicer	
76.	Rockin' Crystals	
77.	Bouncy Quicksand	

Now Try This!

The boys uncovered lots of cool stuff at the museum. See if you can dig up these 10 words from this chapter hidden in this word-search puzzle:

Dino
Quicksand
Geode
Footprint
Ghost
Iceberg
Fossil
Museum
Haunted
Elastomer

```
F O O T P R I N T E
T I C E B E R G E L
H A U N T E D M Q A
F M S A L E O I E S
O Q G H O S T D N T
S D E S S P O U Q O
S R O A M U S E U M
I I D K G D Q I S E
L F E N U A F M O R
Q U I C K S A N D K
```

Be sure to look horizontally, vertically, and diagonally.

Turn to page 136 to check your answers.

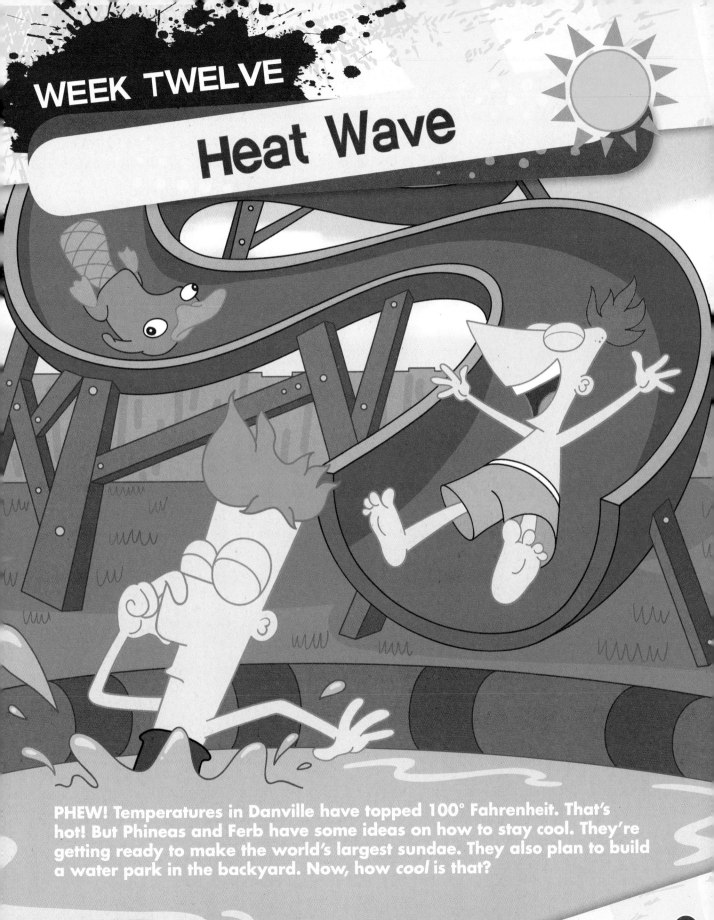

WEEK TWELVE

Heat Wave

PHEW! Temperatures in Danville have topped 100° Fahrenheit. That's hot! But Phineas and Ferb have some ideas on how to stay cool. They're getting ready to make the world's largest sundae. They also plan to build a water park in the backyard. Now, how *cool* is that?

I Scream, You Scream

What better way to chill out than with a cold treat? Phineas and Ferb have drawn up some blueprints for an ice-cream-making machine. But this is no ordinary machine; it can churn out the world's largest ice-cream sundae! Candace, Isabella, and Perry can't wait to try it!

What You Need:

- Small sealable plastic bag
- Large sealable plastic bag
- 2 tablespoons sugar
- 1 cup whole milk
- 1/2 teaspoon vanilla extract
- Ice cubes
- 1/2 cup coarse salt

What You Do:

1. Put the sugar, milk, and vanilla extract into the small bag. Seal it tightly.

2. Add the salt and enough ice to fill half of the large bag. Put the smaller bag inside the larger one. Seal the large bag tightly.

3. Now shake the large bag for about five minutes.

4. Remove the smaller bag. Nice job—you made ice cream!

What's Happening Here?

You learned on page 89 that salt lowers water's freezing point. It causes ice to melt much faster than it normally would. For ice to melt, it must absorb heat from the surrounding environment. Some of the heat comes from the ice-cream mixture. This causes the temperature of the ice-cream mixture to drop. The creamy liquid freezes into solid ice cream. YUM!

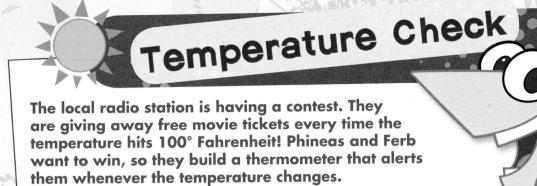

Temperature Check

The local radio station is having a contest. They are giving away free movie tickets every time the temperature hits 100° Fahrenheit! Phineas and Ferb want to win, so they build a thermometer that alerts them whenever the temperature changes.

What You Need:

- Glass jar
- Water
- Clear straw
- Food coloring
- Modeling clay
- Index card
- Scissors
- Pen

What You Do:

1. Fill the jar about three-quarters full of water. Add three drops of food coloring.

2. Dip half the length of the straw into the water. Seal the space between the straw and the top of the bottle with clay. (It must be airtight!)

3. Blow into the straw until water rises halfway up the section of straw sticking out of the bottle.

4. Cut the index card in half. In one of the halves, cut two slits in the middle that are large enough to slide the straw through. See picture.

5. Slide the straw through the card. Use the pen to mark the level of the water in the straw on the card.

6. Set the bottle in a sunny spot. As the temperature heats up, the water rises above the mark you made.

7. Put the bottle in the refrigerator. Watch the water level sink below the mark.

What's Happening Here?

When air inside the bottle heats up, its molecules begin to move faster and push one another farther apart. The expanding air pushes the water out of the way and up the straw. The opposite happens when the thermometer is left in the cold. Air molecules inside the bottle slow down and move closer together. The cooling air shrinks, sucking the water back down the straw.

Sonic Boom

Dr. Doofenshmirtz has made a machine to control people's minds with his voice. He wants to talk everyone into heading outdoors for his birthday party. But Agent P is on the case. He disrupts the waves coming from Dr. Doofenshmirtz's machine with a loud blast of sound. *BANG!*

What You Need:

- Tube from a toilet paper roll
- Index card
- Scissors
- Sharpened pencil
- Plastic wrap
- Rubber band
- Tape
- Paper

What You Do:

1. Trace the end of the tube on the index card. Cut out the circle. Use the pencil to poke a small hole in the circle's center.

2. Tape the circle to one end of the tube.

3. Fit a piece of plastic wrap over the other end of the tube. Wrap a rubber band around the tube to hold the wrap in place. Stretch the plastic wrap so it is pulled tight.

4. Cut a thin strip of paper 5 inches long and no wider than a pencil. Fold the strip about an inch from the end. Tape the folded bit to a flat surface so the rest of the paper sticks up.

5. Point the end of the tube with the hole a few inches from the paper strip. Tap the plastic-wrapped end of the tube. The strip bends!

What's Happening Here?

Invisible sound waves move through the air and bounce off objects. (You learned about this on page 73.) If they are strong enough, they can move things in their path. Tapping the end of the sound tube causes vibrations to travel down the tube. The small hole in the tube's end concentrates the sound waves and aims them at the paper strip. When they hit, the strip wobbles!

Super Soaker

Warning!
You need an adult helper for this project. This project can get messy. Do it outdoors.

To cool off, Phineas and Ferb build a water park in their backyard! There's a huge fountain at the park's center that's making quite a splash. Water gushes out and soars into the air. Let's get soaked!

What You Need:

- Large plastic soda bottle
- Nail
- Balloon
- Water

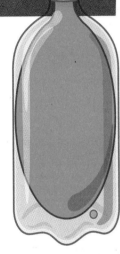

What You Do:

1. Have an adult poke a hole with a nail into the side of plastic soda bottle near its base.

2. Stretch the neck of the balloon over the bottle's mouth and push the balloon into the bottle.

3. Blow into the mouth of the balloon to inflate it inside the bottle. Once inflated, cover the hole in the bottom of the bottle with your finger. This keeps the balloon inflated.

4. Pour water into the mouth of the bottle to fill the balloon. Point the bottle away from you, and remove your finger from the hole. Splash down!

What's Happening Here?

As you inflate the balloon, air molecules in the bottle are pushed out of the hole. This creates a **vacuum**. That's why when you cover the hole with your finger, the balloon stays inflated. Remove the finger, and air flows back into the bottle. This air rushing into the bottle forces the water in the balloon up and out the narrow mouth of the bottle. *Woosh!*

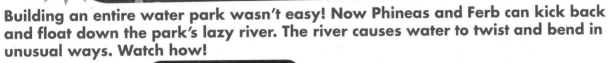

Bendy Water

Building an entire water park wasn't easy! Now Phineas and Ferb can kick back and float down the park's lazy river. The river causes water to twist and bend in unusual ways. Watch how!

What You Need:

- Plastic comb
- Water faucet

What You Do:

1. Comb through your hair several times.

2. Turn the faucet on so there's a gentle and steady stream. Hold the comb near the stream of water. Don't let the comb and water touch! Wow!

What's Happening Here?

The water bends! This is thanks to static electricity. (Remember from page 39?) Combing your hair causes a charge to build up on the comb. When you hold the comb near the water, the charge pulls on the water molecules. It is strong enough to bend the stream!

Slip and Slide

The main attraction at Phineas and Ferb's water park is its water slides. Water blasts riders down the slippery slopes and through loops and tunnels. What a rush! Now try this slippery project.

What You Need:
- Butter
- 3 identical beads
- Straw
- Wooden spoon
- Metal spoon
- Glass
- Warm water

What You Do:

1. Use a dab of butter to stick a bead to the straw and handles of the spoons. Stick the beads so they are positioned at the same height when you stand the utensils in the glass.

2. Fill the glass a quarter full of warm water.

3. Stand the straw and spoons up in the glass. Which bead races down the utensils the fastest?

What's Happening Here?

The winner of this race is the bead on the metal spoon. Metals are good conductors of heat. Heat moves through the metal spoon much faster than through the plastic straw or wooden spoon. When the heat reaches the butter, it starts to melt. The slippery butter reduces friction so the bead can slide toward the finish line. In a similar way, water reduces friction so people can rush down a water slide without sticking. WHEE!

Solar Cookout

Warning!
You need an adult helper for this project.

It's hot enough outside to fry an egg on the sidewalk. That gives Phineas an idea. He and Ferb can use the sun's energy to cook. They put together a device that collects sunlight to heat up food. Slip on a pair of sunglasses and get cooking!

What You Do:

1. Use scissors to cut a flap in the lid of the pizza box. The flap's edge should be 1 inch from the left, right, and front sides of the box top. (Use a ruler to help you.) Do not cut along the back side.

2. Open the flap and line the underside of the flap with foil.

3. Stretch a piece of plastic wrap over the hole in the lid left by your flap. Tape around the edges of the plastic to make a tight seal.

4. Line the inside of the pizza box with foil. Then put a layer of black construction paper on the bottom.

5. Place a marshmallow on a small piece of aluminum foil in the bottom of the box.

6. Close the box lid. Prop open the flap at a right angle with the straw. Use tape to hold the straw in place.

7. Set the box in a sunny spot so sunlight directly hits the foil. Wait till your marshmallow melts! (Be careful, it might be hot!)

What You Need:

- Pizza box
- Scissors
- Ruler
- Foil
- Plastic wrap
- Tape
- Black construction paper
- Marshmallow
- Straw

What's Happening Here?

Solar ovens like the one in this project are used all over the world to cook food. How do they work? Light reflects off the foil on the flap and into the box. This heats up the space inside. The plastic-wrap-covered window allows light to enter the box, but it traps heat inside. This is called the **greenhouse effect**. The black paper absorbs heat and helps keep the cooker hot, so food stays toasty.

This Week's Roundup

Excellent work! Fill in the chart to keep track of the results of your experiments.

EXPERIMENT		DESCRIBE THE RESULTS OF THE EXPERIMENT
78.	I Scream, You Scream	
79.	Temperature Check	
80.	Sonic Boom	
81.	Super Soaker	
82.	Bendy Water	
83.	Slip and Slide	
84.	Solar Cookout	

Now Try This!

Here are some science riddles that are sure to tickle your ulna nerve, or "funny bone." For the punch lines, turn to page 136.

1. Why did the moon stop eating?

2. How do you know the ocean is friendly?

3. What kind of Valentine's Day cards do volcanoes receive?

4. H_2O is the formula for water. So what's the formula for ice?

5. What did one magnet say to the other?

WEEK THIRTEEN

Sports Spectacular

Ferb's cousins are visiting from England. They're sad about missing their favorite soccer team play back home. Phineas has an idea. Why not set up a sporting event in the backyard? He'll call them the Backyard Games! Everyone can compete in all sorts of sports—from swimming to bowling. There'll also be cool medals for the top champs. The Backyard Games won't be all about muscle, though; athletes will also have to use science to win!

Dazzling Arena

Phineas and Ferb design a domed stadium to hold the Backyard Games! They want to make it look extra fancy. They want it to glow with changing colors and lights. Let's check out the light show!

What You Need:
- Large clear plastic lid
- Flashlight
- Tape
- 1/2 cup water
- 1 teaspoon dishwashing liquid
- Bowl
- Spoon
- Straw

What You Do:

1. Tape the plastic lid with its lip facing upward to the top of the flashlight.

2. Mix together the water and dishwashing liquid in a bowl. Put a spoonful of bubble solution on top of the lid.

3. Put the straw into the solution on the lid. Blow a bubble dome big enough to cover the entire lid.

4. Turn on the flashlight and turn off the lights in the room. Watch colors swirl on the bubble's surface!

5. Pop the bubble and remove the flashlight from the lid.

6. Set the lid on a flat surface. Blow two large bubbles of equal size on the lid. Make sure the bubbles are touching each other.

7. Set the flashlight so it shines through the wall between where the two bubbles meet. Look at the wall from different angles. You can see lines of colored bands down the bubbles' wall!

What's Happening Here?

White light is made up of different **wavelengths** of light. Different light waves produce different colors. Remember from page 14 that light is made up of lots of different colors. Some light waves bounce off the soapy bubble's surface, meet up, and combine together. This **interference** creates new colors and amazing swirls and stripes on the bubbles' surfaces.

Bowl-a-Strike!

What's the first sporting event in the Backyard Challenge? It's bowling! Phineas and Ferb have found a way to make the sport really exciting. They've built the world's largest bowling ball and pins. You have to climb inside the ball to steer it! Grab some competitors and bowl!

What You Need:

- 10 markers
- Tennis ball
- 5-foot-long string
- Stapler

What You Do:

1. Arrange the 10 markers on a flat surface. Stand them upright like bowling pins in four rows of one, two, three, and four markers. Space the rows about 2 inches apart.

2. Staple the string to the tennis ball.

3. Hold the string in one hand so the tennis ball is on a level with the center of the "bowling pins." The ball should also be about 1 foot away from the first pin.

4. Use your other hand to pull the string back. Let go. How many pins did you knock over? Challenge your opponents.

What's Happening Here?

The ball on the string acts like a **pendulum**. When a weight on the end of a string is pulled back and let go, gravity causes it to swing forward. Whichever direction you angle the ball in, when released, the pendulum will swing in that direction. For striking results, the farther you pull the ball, the more force it will have to knock over the bowling pins.

Super Strength

Next up in the Backyard Games: arm wrestling! Buford is ready to show off his upper-arm strength. Phineas has been helping him train. He has been making Buford crush soda bottles with his bare hands! *GRRR!* Watch him go.

What You Need:
- Large plastic soda bottle
- Warm water
- Large bowl of ice water

What You Do:

1. Pour warm water into the bottle. Screw on the cap. Swish the water around for a minute.

2. Pour the water out and quickly screw the cap back on.

3. Lay the bottle in the bowl of ice water. Pour some of the ice water over the bottle. The bottle collapses!

What's Happening Here?

Adding warm water to the bottle warms the air inside. The air molecules expand. Plunging the bottle into ice water causes the warm air inside the bottle to quickly cool. The air molecules come together. This lowers the air pressure inside the bottle. The air pressure outside the bottle is much stronger than inside. The pressure difference crushes the bottle! *THUNK!*

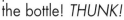

Cereal Surprise

Athletes need to keep their bodies in top physical condition. So Phineas and Ferb have whipped up some health shakes. The only problem is that they taste awful! At least the drinks are packed with vitamins and minerals. Let's check out a strange (but healthy) ingredient in everyday breakfast food.

What You Need:

- 2 cups cereal with large flakes and 100 percent of the recommended daily allowance of iron (Check the label!)
- Large sealable bag
- Strong magnet
- Warm water

What You Do:

1. Put the cereal in the bag. Fill the bag half full of water.

2. Seal the bag and make sure it doesn't leak. Let it sit for 20 minutes.

3. Shake the bag until the cereal-water mixture looks like soup.

4. Place the magnet underneath the bag so it touches the plastic. Slowly slosh the cereal around for a couple of minutes with the magnet in place.

5. Flip the bag over with the magnet still touching. Move the magnet to a spot on the bag where there's an air pocket.

6. Do you see tiny black specks near the magnet? That's iron! Move the magnet and the iron follows.

What's Happening Here?

Most breakfast cereals are **fortified** with this iron. Magnets allow you to see the iron in cereal because they attract this metal (see page 30). Iron is an important mineral that keeps your body healthy. It is part of a compound found in red blood cells. These blood cells carry oxygen from your lungs to the rest of your body. Your body contains the same amount of iron as in two small nails!

Speedy Swimmers

Everyone has suited up for a swimming competition! Isabella's backstroke can't be beat. She's sure she'll win this event. Or will she? Check out these speedy swimmers.

What You Need:

- Construction paper
- Scissors
- Large rectangular pan
- Water
- Dishwashing liquid

What You Do:

1. Cut two triangles out of the paper. These will be your swimmers.

2. Fill the pan with water. Carefully place your swimmers on the water side by side near one end of the pan.

3. Have a friend squeeze a large drop of dishwashing liquid onto his or her index finger. You do the same, too.

4. Each of you choose a triangle. On the count of three, touch the dishwashing liquid on the fingers to the water behind the chosen swimmer. *Zoom!*

What's Happening Here?

You learned on page 28 about a property of water called surface tension. Water molecules like to bond together. But dishwashing liquid weakens these bonds. Touching a drop of soap behind a swimmer decreases the surface tension. The surface tension in front of the swimmer remains strong, though. That pulls the swimmer forward.

Secret Message

Warning!
You need an adult helper for this project.

Agent P has been monitoring the games to make sure it goes without a hitch. Suddenly, he gets a note from Major Monogram. It's so secret, it's written in invisible ink. Reveal the message!

What You Need:

- Lemon
- Water
- Bowl
- Cotton swab
- White paper
- Lamp with an incandescent lightbulb (Do NOT use halogen, fluorescent, or LED bulbs.)

What You Do:

1. Squeeze the juice of half a lemon into a bowl and add a few drops of water.

2. Dip the cotton swab into the juice. Use the swab to write a message on the paper.

3. Let the message dry completely.

4. Have an adult hold the paper up to a lamp until the message appears. Do not touch the paper to the bulb. (Be careful, lightbulbs can get very hot.)

What's Happening Here?

Incandescent lightbulbs produce heat as well as light. The heat given off by the lamp warms the lemon juice on the paper. This causes any water in the juice to evaporate. The compounds that remain react with the air and **oxidize**. This causes the lemon juice to turn from clear to brown.

Acid Test

The secret message was about Dr. Doofenshmirtz. He has made an acid that will eat a hole in the boys' stadium. Agent P needs to find a chemical that will stop the acid.

What You Need:
- 1/2 cup blackberries
- Sealable plastic bag
- 1/4 cup water
- Bowl
- Scissors
- Coffee filter
- Paper towels
- 3 different household liquids (for example: vinegar, milk, seltzer water, dishwashing detergent)

What You Do:

1. Place the berries in the bag. Squeeze the air out and seal it.

2. Mash the berries in the bag until they look like jam. Plop the mush into a bowl. Then add water to the bowl.

3. Cut your coffee filter into strips the size of a stick of gum. Soak the strips in the berry mix.

4. Remove the strips and scrape off any berry bits. Lay the strips on paper towels to completely dry.

5. Dip the dried strips into household liquids. Color change!

Warning! Some of the ingredients used can stain. Cover your work area with a newspaper.

What's Happening Here?

Blackberries contain a chemical that reacts with acids and bases, causing them to change color. Acids contain hydrogen ions and bases contain hydroxide ions. The juice strips detect the amounts of these ions in a liquid (a liquid's **pH**). The strips turn red in acids and purple in bases. Acids and bases **neutralize** each other. Which household liquid should Agent P use to stop Doofenshmirtz's acid?

Cool! You've completed another week of projects! Fill in the chart to keep track of the results of your experiments.

EXPERIMENT	DESCRIBE THE RESULTS OF THE EXPERIMENT
85. Dazzling Arena	
86. Bowl-a-Strike!	
87. Super Strength	
88. Cereal Surprise	
89. Speedy Swimmers	
90. Secret Message	
91. Acid Test	

Now Try This!

Help Perry decode a secret message from Major Monogram. Use the key below. Each number in the bottom row represents the letter directly above it in the top row. To find the answer, turn to page 136.

A	B	C	D	E	F	G	H	I	J	K	L
8	7	1	11	15	2	21	4	12	23	17	26

M	N	O	P	Q	R	S	T	U	V	W	X	Y	Z
9	14	24	22	3	13	18	6	20	25	10	19	16	5

```
__   T    __   __        __   __
18   6    24   22        11   13

__   __   __   F    __   __   __   __   __   __   __   T    _!
11   24   24   2    15   14   18   4    9    12   13   6    5
```

WEEK FOURTEEN

Superstars

Should Phineas and Ferb make a movie this week or join a band? Why not do both? First they are going to direct a horror film—starring Candace! It's going to have some great scary scenes, so get ready! Then Phineas, Ferb, and Baljeet tune up their instruments. Their band, Phineas and the Ferb-Tones, is going to put on a concert. Get ready to rock!

Lights, Camera, Action!

Who are the hottest new directors in town? Phineas and Ferb! They've been making movies on a set in their backyard. Their next film is an action-packed monster movie. While the boys are busy planning the chase scene, let's check on the camera.

What You Need:

- Tall cardboard canister with lid (A potato-chip can works great!)
- Waxed paper
- Scissors
- Pushpin
- Duct tape

Warning!
You need an adult helper for this project.

What You Do:

1. Have an adult cut the cardboard can in two at about 2 inches from the bottom.

2. Trace the bottom of the can onto waxed paper. Cut out the circle.

3. Stack together the bottom half of the can, its lid, the paper circle, and the top of the can. Then put duct tape around where everything meets to seal the parts together.

4. Have an adult use the pushpin to make a small hole in the center of the can's bottom.

5. Hold the open end of the can up to your eye. Cup your hands around the opening to block out any light. Point the other end at a bright image (one lit by sunlight works best, but avoid looking directly at the sun with your camera). You see the image upside down!

What's Happening Here?

The viewer you made is called a **camera obscura**. Light passes through the tiny hole in the bottom of the camera and projects an image onto the waxed paper. Your eye works in the same way. Light shines through your **pupil** and projects an image on the back of your eyeball. Light travels in straight lines. So light rays from the top and bottom of an image cross as they enter the camera's pinhole. Now the top of the image is on the bottom, and the bottom is on top! Just like the camera, the image your eyes see is also flipped! Your brain rights the image so the world doesn't look upside down!

Moving Pictures

Candace wants to star in Phineas and Ferb's film. But she doesn't realize it's a horror movie. The boys transform their leading lady into a werewolf. Wait until she sees herself on film! Check out how film works.

What You Need:
- Index card
- Scissors
- Markers
- 2 rubber bands

What You Do:

1. Cut out a circle from the index card.

2. In the center of one side of the card, draw a goldfish. On the other side of the card, draw a fishbowl. The fishbowl should be large enough for the goldfish to fit inside.

3. Poke a hole in the circle to the right and left of the goldfish and fishbowl. Thread a rubber band through a hole. Tuck the threaded end through the loop at the other end of the rubber band and pull. Do the same to fasten the rubber band on the other side of the circle.

4. Hold one rubber band in each hand and twist the card. Let go. As the card spins, the fish appears inside the bowl!

What's Happening Here?

Even after an image disappears, your eyes still see the image for a short time. That's why the two images on either side of the card seem to overlap as they flip back and forth. Movies trick your eyes in the same way. A series of images flash on the movie screen. Each one is slightly different than the one before it. Most movies flicker images up on the screen at a rate of 24 times per second! The images combine together so you see a moving picture.

Gross Out

To make their movie extra scary, Phineas and Ferb mix up a batch of fake blood. For the effect to look real, they have to get the color and thickness of the gory stuff just right. Here's the recipe they used!

Warning!
This project is messy. Food coloring can stain. Don't perform this experiment without an adult's permission.

What You Need:

- 1/4 cup water
- 1 cup corn syrup
- 2 tablespoons cornstarch
- 2 tablespoons powdered cocoa
- Red food coloring
- Bowl
- Spoon
- White paper towel

What You Do:

1. Mix the water, corn syrup, cornstarch, cocoa, and a few drops of red food coloring in the bowl.

2. Drip some of the blood onto your skin and onto the paper towel. How realistic does it look?

What's Happening Here?

You learned on page 113 that red blood contain iron. This metal gives blood its red color. When iron reacts with the air, it oxidizes and **rusts**, turning brown. That's why the most realistic-looking fake blood is actually reddish-brown. The chocolate syrup and food coloring help re-create this color. Real blood also isn't **transparent** or runny. In the recipe, cornstarch helps make the blood not appear see-through. The corn syrup helps thicken it up.

Rubber Band

Nobody likes to rock out more than Phineas and Ferb. That's why they've put together their own band to make some awesome music! Before they can jam, they need to get their instruments ready. Phineas is going to play the guitar. Give him a hand in putting it together!

What You Need:
- Shoe box
- Pencil
- Scissors
- 8 paper clips
- 4 rubber bands of different thicknesses

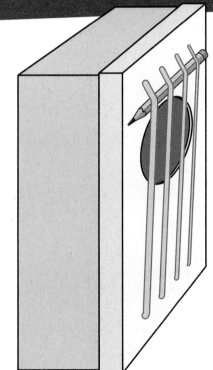

What You Do:

1. Cut a 4-inch-wide hole toward one end of the shoe box's lid.

2. Use the point of the pencil to poke a row of four holes near one end of the shoe box's top. Poke another row of four holes at the opposite end of the box. The holes at each end should line up.

3. Cut each rubber band in half. Tie one end to a paper clip.

4. Thread the thinnest rubber band through an outside hole from beneath the top of the box.

5. Stretch the rubber band across the box top and thread it through its opposite hole. On the inside of the box top, tie the end of the rubber band to another paper clip. The rubber band shouldn't be loose. If it is, trim some off and retie it.

6. Repeat steps 4 and 5 for the remaining rubber bands. Put the rubber bands in order from thinnest to thickest.

7. Slide the pencil under the rubber bands next to the row of holes closest to the large hole in the box top.

8. You've made a guitar! Pluck the strings to see how it sounds.

What's Happening Here?

Plucking the rubber bands on your guitar causes them to vibrate and produce sound waves. Each rubber band makes a sound with a different **pitch**. Thicker bands produce a lower sound because they vibrate more slowly. Thinner bands vibrate faster and have a higher sound. If you press down on a rubber band while plucking it, you can also change its pitch.

Whistling a Tune

Ferb needs an instrument to play. It's got to have a cool sound. He tries out lots of instruments, but none will do. So Ferb decides to make his own sliding whistle.

What You Need:

- Straw (straight, not bendy)
- Scissors
- Glass of water

What's Happening Here?

Air blowing over the top of the long portion of the straw creates sound waves. As you move the straw up and down in the glass, different portions become filled with air and water. Just like with the guitar in the previous experiment, this changes the whistle's pitch. More air in the tube produces sound waves with a lower **frequency** and pitch. Less air in the tube makes sound waves with a higher frequency and pitch.

What You Do:

1. About 2 inches from the top of the straw, cut a slit. (Don't cut the entire way through the straw!) Bend the part above the slit down to make a right angle with the rest of the straw.

2. Set the long part of the straw in the glass of water. Hold the top of the long section.

3. Put your lips on the opening of the short bent section and blow. It whistles! Move the straw up and down in the water to change the sound.

Noisemaker

Baljeet has joined the band, too. He will be wailing on a kazoo. Check out how his kazoo sounds.

What You Need:

- 2 Popsicle sticks
- 1 wide rubber band
- 2 narrower rubber bands
- Straw
- Scissors

What's Happening Here?

Blowing through the kazoo makes the rubber band vibrate. That makes a buzzing sound. The harder you blow, the louder the buzzing will be. If you slide the straws closer to the center of the kazoo, you'll shorten how much of the rubber band can vibrate. That will raise the pitch.

What You Do:

1. Wrap the wide rubber band lengthwise around a Popsicle stick.

2. Cut two ½-inch pieces from the straw. Slide one piece under the rubber band near one end of the Popsicle stick.

3. Set the second piece of straw on the opposite end. This time the straw should be on top of the rubber band. Set the other Popsicle stick on top of the straws.

4. Wrap a narrow rubber band around one end of the sticks to pinch them together. Wrap the remaining rubber band around the other end.

5. Put your mouth in the middle of the sticks and blow. You'll hear a *BZZZ!*

Light Show

The band is ready to go! It's time to hear Phineas and the Ferb-Tones live in concert! Isabella is in charge of lighting the stage. She's set up a flashing spotlight that moves to the music. That will really make this concert rock!

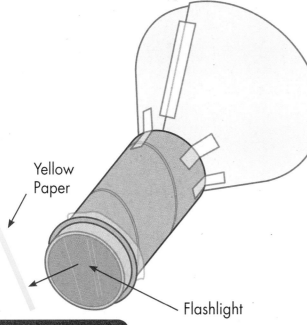

Yellow Paper

Flashlight

What You Need:

- Cardboard tube from a toilet paper roll
- Plastic wrap
- Rubber band
- Sheet of plain white paper
- Tape
- Yellow construction paper
- Flashlight

What You Do:

1. Stretch a piece of plastic wrap over one end of the tube. Hold it in place with a rubber band. Make sure the plastic wrap is completely smooth.

2. Roll the white paper into a cone with about an inch-wide opening at its smaller end. Tape the cone so it doesn't unroll.

3. Push the small end of the cone into the open end of the cardboard tube until it fits snuggly in place. Tape the cone to the tube.

4. Tape the yellow paper to a wall. Lay the tube so the plastic-wrapped end is pointed at the paper. Lay the flashlight so it is pointed at the plastic wrap. Angle the flashlight until you see a spot of light appear on the yellow paper.

5. Loudly shout or sing into the cone. The spot of light dances around!

What's Happening Here?

Sound waves are invisible, but this project lets you see your own voice! Speaking into the cone vibrates the plastic wrap on the end of the tube. The light from the flashlight bounces off the vibrating plastic. You can see its shimmering pattern reflected onto the paper.

You rock! Fill in the chart to keep track of the results of your experiments.

	EXPERIMENT	DESCRIBE THE RESULTS OF THE EXPERIMENT
92.	Lights, Camera, Action!	
93.	Moving Pictures	
94.	Gross Out	
95.	Rubber Band	
96.	Whistling a Tune	
97.	Noisemaker	
98.	Light Show	

Now Try This!

See if you can unscramble the words below. All the jumbled words can be found in this chapter. For answers, go to page 136.

1. OAZOK _ _ _ _ _

2. VEMIO _ _ _ _ _

3. QUEENCFYR _ _ _ _ _ _ _ _ _

4. KEAF DOLOB _ _ _ _ _ _ _ _ _

5. FLOWREEW _ _ _ _ _ _ _ _

6. SLIHWET _ _ _ _ _ _ _

Unscramble all the highlighted letters above to answer the top secret question below.

The Secret Question: What's the name of Phineas and Ferb's band?

Phineas and the _ _ _ _ - _ _ _ _ _

WEEK FIFTEEN

Time Travel

It's been an exciting summer and Phineas and Ferb aren't ready for it to be over just yet. There's only one thing to do! They're going to build a time machine to travel back to the first day of summer. Then they can start the fun all over again. But time travel is tricky! Will the boys end up in the right time? Let's find out.

FIRST DAY OF SUMMER

Penny Power

It's going to take a lot of power to travel all the way back to the beginning of summer. While Phineas gets to work designing a time machine, Ferb starts collecting the needed parts. He knows they'll need a battery with a lot of *oomph* to run their time-traveling device. Let's see if this one works.

What You Need:

- Bowl
- 1/4 cup white vinegar
- 1 tablespoon salt
- 6 pennies dated before 1982
- Permanent marker
- Aluminum foil
- Paper towel
- Scissors
- 2 pieces of copper wire with stripped ends
- Tape
- Paper plate
- Small LED bulb from a string of holiday lights

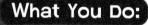

What You Do:

1. Mix the salt and vinegar together in the bowl.

2. Trace around a penny to draw six circles on the aluminum foil and six on the paper towel. Cut out the circles. Place the paper towel circles in the bowl.

3. Tape one end of a wire to a foil circle and place it on the paper plate, wire side down.

4. Stack a wet paper circle on top of the foil circle. Next stack a penny on top. Continue layering in this order: foil, paper, and penny. Wrap tape around the stack to secure it.

5. Tape the second wire to your last penny. Wind the opposite ends of the wires around each prong of the LED. (You might have to switch which wire connects to which prong to see a result.) The LED lights up!

What's Happening Here?

A battery uses a chemical reaction to produce electricity. The vinegar-and-salt mixture is an **electrolyte**. This is a liquid that contains electrically charged ions. Metals in the penny and foil react with the electrolyte to release electrons. You may have noticed that store-bought batteries have a positive and a negative end. In your battery, the penny is the negative end and the foil is the positive end. The electrons flow through the wires in a **circuit**, from the negative to the positive end of the battery. Along the way, they light up your LED!

Juiced Up

Oh no! The time machine isn't working! It needs more power. If the boys' time machine runs out of energy, they could get stuck in the past. Time to test a new battery to see if it can help ramp up the machine!

What You Need:

- Lemon
- Plate
- 2 pennies dated before 1982
- 2 galvanized nails
- 3 pieces of copper wire with stripped ends
- Headphones

What You Do:

1. Have an adult cut the lemon in half. Set the halves cut-side down on a plate.

2. Stick a penny and a nail into either side of each lemon half.

3. Wrap one end of a copper wire around a nail. On the same lemon half, wrap a second copper wire around the penny. Connect this wire to the nail on the other lemon half.

4. Wrap the last piece of wire around the remaining penny.

5. Put the headphones on. Touch the ends of the wires from your lemon battery to the headphone jack. (Make sure not to get the jack wet to avoid damaging the headphones.) The crackling you hear is electricity!

What's Happening Here?

Each lemon half in this project is a battery. They work just like the stacked penny-foil battery in the previous experiment. Instead of vinegar and salt, these batteries' electrolyte is lemon juice! By connecting two batteries together in a **series**, you can get twice the electricity.

Bending Light

The time machine is finally ready. Phineas and Ferb climb in and program it to bring them back to the first day of summer. They start the machine. WHOA! There's a loud explosion and they are pulled into a swirling tunnel of light. Everything is bending—even light. See what this looks like.

What You Need:
- Large plastic soda bottle
- Scissors
- Tape
- Milk
- Water
- Flashlight
- Black construction paper

What You Do:

1. Have an adult use scissors to poke a hole in the side of the bottle, near the bottom. Cover the hole with a piece of tape.

2. Put a few drops of milk in the bottle. Then fill the rest with water. The liquid inside should look cloudy.

3. Set the bottle on a counter with the hole pointed at a sink.

4. Cut a piece of construction paper that is large enough to cover the face of the flashlight. Make a small hole in the center of the paper; this will allow some light to come through. Tape the cover in place.

5. Position the flashlight on the side of the soda bottle opposite the hole. Aim the light so it will shine through the hole on the other side.

6. Turn out the overhead lights to make the room as dark as possible. Remove the tape from the hole. The light bends with the stream of water!

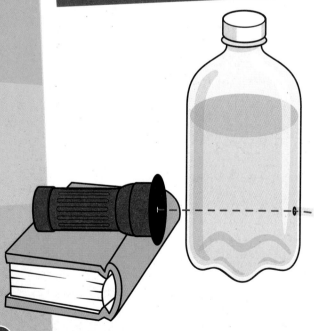

What's Happening Here?

Light travels only in straight lines. But this project makes light appear to bend. How? The light never makes it out of the hole in a straight line because it gets trapped in the stream. Water reflects light. As water pours out of the bottle, light shining through the hole bounces back and forth off the sides of the stream of water as it curves. The result: The light looks like it bends.

Joust About

Wait a minute! This doesn't look like Danville at all. Phineas and Ferb's time traveling has gone off course—by several hundred years! Knights in the middle of a jousting tournament surround their time machine. Why not stick around and join the action?

What You Need:
- Non-bendy plastic straw
- Potato

What You Do:
1. Set the potato on a flat surface.
2. Hold the straw and try to jab it into the potato. What happens?
3. Now use your thumb to cover one end of the straw.
4. Jab the potato again. See the difference?

What's Happening Here?

In jousting, knights on horseback use a long pole called a lance to knock their opponent out of their seat. A straw is a pretty flimsy excuse for a lance. But with your thumb over the straw's end, that's a different story. As you jab into the potato, trapped air fills up the straw. This keeps the straw stiff so it pierces the potato! Uncovered, the air flows right through the straw.

Gyrocopter

Phineas and Ferb try to flash forward, traveling back to their own time. Oops. They overshot! They wind up in the future. The boys are excited to find people flying around in cool spaceships. Check out this spinning model.

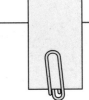

What You Need:
- Paper
- Ruler
- Scissors
- Paper clip

What You Do:
1. Cut a 1.5-inch-by-6.5-inch strip of paper.
2. Starting at one end, cut a 3-inch slit down the middle of the strip to make two flaps.
3. Fold the flaps down in opposite directions. Your flyer's shape should look like the letter T.
4. Slide a paper clip onto the bottom of the flyer.
5. Raise your arm as high as you can and drop the flyer. Whoa! It spins to the ground!

What's Happening Here?

You made an **autogyro**, a type of aircraft with blades that spin on their own. When you drop the autogyro, gravity pulls it down. The flaps act like wings to help keep the flyer in the air. But as the flyer falls, air bends the edges of the wings up at opposite angles. This causes the flyer to start spinning. Adding the paper clip helps **stabilize** the autogyro so it falls straight down instead of tumbling in the air.

Big Kaboom

The time machine has just enough power for one more trip. Let's hope Phineas and Ferb get it right this time. Fingers crossed! This time the machine takes off with a loud blast. Try this final project for an amazing, exploding send-off to summer!

Warning!
This project is messy. Do it outdoors. Wear goggles to protect your eyes.

What You Need:
- Small plastic bottle of diet cola
- 3 Mentos candies
- 2 Index cards

What's Happening Here?

You can't see them, but there are tiny pits covering the surface of a candy. These **nucleation sites** are great for attracting bubbles of carbon dioxide trapped in soda. The second the Mentos fall into the soda and sink to the bottom, bubbles begin to form all over the candy. This triggers the gas dissolved in the soda to rush out of the drink. The gas speeds toward the top of the bottle. Any liquid in the way gets pushed out the top like a fountain. *KABOOM!*

What You Do:

1. Open the soda and set it on the ground.

2. Roll one index card into a tube so you can stack three pieces of the candies inside. Place another index card underneath.

3. Set the candy-filled tube and card over the opening of the soda bottle. Line the tube up with the top of the bottle.

4. Get ready to move out of the way! Quickly pull the card out from under the tube so the candies fall into the bottle. The soda explodes sky high!

This Week's Roundup

Congratulations, you finished all 104 experiments in this book!
Fill in the chart to keep track of the results of your experiments.

EXPERIMENT	DESCRIBE THE RESULTS OF THE EXPERIMENT
99. Penny Power	
100. Juiced Up	
101. Bending Light	
102. Joust About	
103. Gyrocopter	
104. Big Kaboom	

Now Try This!

For the grand finale, complete this crossword puzzle! All the clues can be
found in this chapter! Need answers? Turn to page 136.

Across

1. Liquid that contains ions

2. _____ travel

3. Power source for TV remote control

4. Aircraft supported by wings that rotate under their own power

Down

5. Ancient armor wearer

6. A closed loop that allows electricity to flow

7. When light bounces off a surface

8. The opposite of negative

9. Type of lightbulb found in some holiday lights

10. A spud

The End?

What happened to Phineas and Ferb? Did they make it back or are they still stuck in the future?

When the time machine stops, the boys get out and have a look around. PHEW, this looks familiar. The boys have landed smack-dab in the middle of their backyard right under the tree. And it's exactly 104 days in the past. They made it back and summer is just beginning! HOORAY!

There's just one thing about time travel that Phineas and Ferb forgot to consider. By traveling back to the start of summer vacation, they are going to bump into their past selves. They run into them just as the old Phineas and Ferb are discussing their first summer project—the bubble-making machine!

Talk about seeing double! With two sets of brothers, Candace won't know which pair to bust first! Two Phineases and two Ferbs equal twice the fun. Now they can build bigger and better projects. When the summer is over (again), the time-traveling Phineas and Ferb can get some help repairing their time machine to return home.

This really will be THE BEST SUMMER EVER!

Glossary

acid: Material that is usually characterized as having a sour taste. Acids contain an excess of hydrogen ions.

adhesion: When molecules of different substances stick together

air pressure: Force of air pushing against a surface

airfoil: Curved shape of a wing

amplify: To increase the volume of sound

atom: Smallest possible particle of a chemical element

autogyro: Aircraft supported by wings that rotate under their own power

axis: Imaginary line about which an object rotates

ballast tank: Tank within a ship that holds water or air

base: Any chemical compound that gives off negatively charged hydroxide ions when dissolved in water. Bases react with acids to form neutral substances.

Bernoulli's principle: The principle that states that an increase in the speed of a stream of air results in a decrease in pressure

buoyancy: Upward force that a fluid exerts on an object

camera obscura: Device used to project an upside-down image

capillary action: When a trapped liquid rises through a tiny tube. This is due to surface tension.

center of gravity: Point where the entire weight of an object is balanced

centripetal force: Force that makes an object follow a curved path

chromatography: Separation of a mixture by passing it through a material

circuit: Electricity flowing through a closed loop

cohesion: When molecules of the same substance stick together

conductor: Material that electricity or heat passes through easily

convection: Movement of heat in a liquid or gas

convex lens: Lens that bulges outward used to magnify objects

compost: Plant fertilizer made of decayed plants or other organic matter

crystal: Solid whose molecules are organized in a regular repeating pattern

decompose: To break down chemically into simpler components

density: Amount of mass in a given unit

desiccation: The act of drying out

diffusion: The act of spreading out

displace: To push aside

dissolve: To become incorporated into a liquid

drag: Slowing force caused by a gas or liquid rubbing over a surface

elastomer: Polymer with elastic properties

electrolysis: Chemical change caused by an electrical current passing through a liquid containing ions

electrolyte: Liquid that contains ions

electrons: Negatively charged particles in an atom

electroscope: Instrument for detecting electricity

evaporate: To turn from a liquid to a gas

force: Push or pull upon an object

forensics: Scientific techniques used to investigate crimes

fortified: Food enriched with nutrients, such as vitamins and minerals

fossil: Preserved remains or impressions of an organism

freezing point: Temperature at which a liquid turns into a solid

frequency: Number of vibrations in a sound or light wave per unit of time

friction: Resistance to movement when two objects rub together

fulcrum: Point on which a lever pivots

fungus: A type of organism that reproduces by spores, such as mold or yeast

geode: Hollow rocks that contain mineral crystals inside

gravity: Attractive force that pulls two objects together

greenhouse effect: When the sun's warmth is trapped inside a transparent barrier or by the atmosphere

inertia: Tendency of an object to resist change in its motion

interference: When two waves combine to form a bigger wave or cancel each other out

ion: Charged particle

kinetic energy: Energy of motion

lift: Upward force

load: Force applied to a structure

magnetic field: Area around a magnet where magnetic force is applied

mass: Amount of matter in an object

mechanical energy: Energy of motion used to perform work

microbe: Microscopic single-celled or multicellular organism

mineral: Natural nonliving solid that makes up rocks

miscible: Being capable of being mixed

molecule: Neutral group of two or more atoms

neutralize: To make a chemical neutral, like when an acid and base mix

non-Newtonian fluid: Substance that has properties of both a liquid and a solid

nucleation site: Site on the surface of an object where a gas, liquid, or solid forms

orbit: Curved path of a planet or a spacecraft around another space object

oxidize: To change through a reaction to oxygen

pendulum: Weight suspended from a pivoting point

pH: Measure of how acidic or basic a liquid is

photosynthesis: Process plants use to turn sunlight, carbon dioxide, and water into food

pitch: Quality of sound related to the frequency of sound waves. It describes how high or low a note sounds.

polar molecule: Molecule with two different charges on either end that allow it to cling to other molecules

polymer: Substance made of long, chainlike molecules

potential energy: Energy stored by an object

pressure: Force applied over an area

protons: Positively charged particles in an atom

pupil: A small opening at the front of the eye that allows light to enter

reflect: To bounce light off a surface

refract: To change the direction of a beam of light

rust: A reddish-brown flaky coating that forms when iron oxidizes

sediment: Solid material, such as gravel and sand, deposited by water, wind, or glaciers

series: An arrangement of components in a circuit connecting along a single path

solar oven: Device that uses sunlight as its energy source to cook food

sound waves: Vibrations that travel through the air

spore: The reproductive unit of a fungus

stabilize: To keep an object from overturning

stalactite: Tapering structure hanging from the roof of a cave

stalagmite: Tapering column rising from the floor of a cave

static electricity: Electrical charge produced by friction

surface area: How much exposed area a solid's surface has

surface tension: Attraction of the molecules in the surface layer of a liquid

suspension cable: Hanging cable that supports a bridge

tension: Type of pulling force

thrust: Forward force

trajectory: The curved path of a flying object

transparent: See-through

truss: Arrangement of supports beneath a bridge

vacuum: Space that doesn't contain any matter

verdigris: Bluish-green crust that forms when copper oxidizes

vortex: Spinning mass of liquid or air

wavelength: Distance between a light wave's peaks

Puzzle Answers

Page 18

1. Major Monogram; 2. forensics; 3. bubble; 4. density;
5. rainbow; 6. evaporate; The Secret Question: Fireside Girls

Page 26

Across: 1. pasta; 2. float; 3. fungus; 4. Danville
Down: 5. carbon; 6. plastic; 7. acid; 8. flying; 9. energy; 10. lift

Page 34

Page 50

1. A Tyrannosaurus *wrecks*. 2. So they won't be spotted.
3. A rocket. 4. Flying *saucers*. 5. They don't have the guts.

Page 58

1. c 2. d 3. a 4. e 5. b

Page 66

Across: 1. force; 2. atom; 3. coaster; 4. flat; 5. park
Down: 6. hydrogen; 7. gravity; 8. metal; 9. conductor; 10. beast

Page 76

Page 84

1. London; 2. balloon; 3. microbe; 4. lightning;
5. penny; 6. Eiffel Tower; Secret Question: Reginald

Page 100

Page 108

1. It was *full*. 2. It *waves*. 3. Ones that say, "I *lava* you!"
4. H_2O *cubed*! 5. You're very *attractive*.

Page 116

Stop Dr. Doofenshmirtz!

Page 124

1. kazoo; 2. movie; 3. frequency; 4. fake blood;
5. werewolf; 6. whistle; Secret Question: Ferb-Tones

Page 131

Across: 1. electrolyte; 2. time; 3. battery; 4. autogyro
Down: 5. knight; 6. circuit; 7. reflect; 8. positive;
9. LED; 10. potato